The Controversial Issues Being Faced in Education

The Controversial Issues Being Faced in Education

The Pros and Cons Being Encountered in Today's Schools

M. Scott Norton

ROWMAN & LITTLEFIELD
Lanham • Boulder • New York • London

Published by Rowman & Littlefield
An imprint of The Rowman & Littlefield Publishing Group, Inc.
4501 Forbes Boulevard, Suite 200, Lanham, Maryland 20706
www.rowman.com

6 Tinworth Street, London SE11 5AL, United Kingdom

Copyright © 2019 by M. Scott Norton

All rights reserved. No part of this book may be reproduced in any form or by any electronic or mechanical means, including information storage and retrieval systems, without written permission from the publisher, except by a reviewer who may quote passages in a review.

British Library Cataloguing in Publication Information Available

Library of Congress Cataloging-in-Publication Data Available

978-1-4758-5042-0 (cloth)
978-1-4758-5043-7 (pbk)
978-1-4758-5044-4 (electronic)

Contents

Foreword		vii
Preface		ix
	Introduction	1
1	Controversial Issues Being Encountered in Education at the Local Level: Part I	3
2	Controversial Issues Being Encountered in Education at the Local Level: Part II	31
3	Educational Controversies at the State Level	59
4	Educational Controversies at the Federal Level	85
About the Author		113

Foreword

WHAT THE BEST PARENTS WANT FOR THEIR CHILD, WE MUST PROVIDE FOR ALL CHILDREN

These are unusual times. American society and American culture, with their emphasis on speed, quick fixes, and decisive action, have been shaken from their typical routines. Our many freedoms have given each individual the freedom to think, speak, and differ on the many aspects of life.

Assumptions and questions about the American education system and one's roles and commitment to core values may be challenged. It is apparent that we are still dealing with many of the same issues that have faced us historically, but things simply are not what they used to be. The world has changed, and with it there has developed a willingness on the part of many to reconcile what we are believing and doing and why we are doing it. Questions about what is right about the purposes of education are planted in everyday conversations, intellectual debates, and troublesome controversies. What is education all about?

No subject in recent times has received as much attention as has the state of education. It is a time when the future of our children and youth, and therefore our nation, is first and foremost on the minds of our citizenry. One point of agreement is the opportunity for each and every child to reach his or her greatest potential. Yet, controversies are ongoing about just how to best achieve that goal.

At this time, the American citizenry has become less cohesive around the primary educational issues.

What should be taught at the K–12 school levels, how should it be taught, and who should teach it are often open for debate. The events of school choice, student violence, state and national standards, grading practices, teacher performance, vouchers, redshirting, cursive writing, prayer in schools, and many other controversial topics have caused us to reconsider our educational provisions and practices.

Adopting a reflective posture of education seems especially appropriate for the times. Asking fundamental questions is essential for those of us who have a primary concern for the quality of our school programs and the success of all students. Although we have differences, we must give priority to finding best solutions. Best solutions are often found in the efforts given to reliable and valid research combined with the nation's best thinking.

Schooling then becomes a microcosm for the world around us—a place to learn the necessary academics, but also about the richness of the human condition. These qualities come from one's experiences in living, our educational opportunities, and working with others. In our pursuit of academic excellence, we must not forget the human child and the need to provide the foundation for the richness that life has to offer. As we review the data to measure student and education success, it looms important for us to examine our purposes and not lose sight of the faces of our students. Our children, as adults, will become the sum of all they learn as children.

While viewing the differences that are certain to exist in a democracy that favors individualism, free speech, and equity in educational opportunities, the thoughts of the very best educators, teachers, parents, and other citizens must be devoted to the very best education solutions. For what the best of these persons want for their children and youth, we must want for all students.

Barry L. Fritz, EdM
Educator, Principal, and Learning Leader
Broadmor Elementary School
Tempe Elementary School District No. 3, Arizona

Preface

WHY THIS BOOK WAS WRITTEN

School choice, vouchers, prayer in schools, curricular content, online education, sex education, inclusiveness, cursive writing, student grading, racial desegregation, and redshirting are representative of the many major controversial issues encountered in schools today. The teaching of evolution, going green, educational standards, teacher performance pay, guns in schools, teacher licensure, student homework, student grading, busing for segregation, open classrooms, and funding are other differences that are operating within the walls of American's schools.

Such controversies inhibit program operations and student learning in many important ways. The development of a viable curricular program, preparing knowledgeable and skilled educational personnel, engaging student learners, loss of instructional time, inhibiting financial support, severing of positive school/community relationships, and loss of effective school personnel are among the many program factors that are endangered by the presence of ongoing debates. Understanding the controversial issues that are being encountered in education at the local, state, and federal levels of government serves to reveal the major challenges facing school personnel and underscores the paramount importance for engaging the talents of individuals for helping to resolve them.

Thus, the primary purpose of the book is to identify the specific controversial issues at hand and inform the reader about the pros and cons being encountered in each issue along with any valid research and empirical evidence that might serve toward controversial resolutions.

Introduction

HOW THIS BOOK IS ORGANIZED

The four chapters of the book include the major educational controversies/debates that are being encountered currently in local school education. Chapter 1 centers on the controversial educational issues being encountered at the local school level and the debates that tend to inhibit school success. The number of controversial issues at the local level is so extensive that a second chapter also is devoted to issues at the local school level. Chapter 3 focuses on the educational controversies that are primarily a concern of the various states. Chapter 4 focuses on the many controversial education issues being encountered at the federal level of our nation. In each chapter of the book, the nature of the controversies/debates that are present is discussed along with the pro and con statements that underscore the opinion differences that exist among the educators and general citizenry.

Whenever valid and reliable research is available on any issue being discussed, it is included in the discussion. The content does point out, however, the lack of scientific and empirical research in many areas of educational practice. Improved educational research practices at all levels of government are viewed as a significant need for resolving many of the controversies that remain unresolved. The need for extensive educational research is noted throughout the book. In addition, the fact is that almost every educational controversy is present within all three levels of government: local, state, and federal.

All educators, school board members, state department education officials, federal education department personnel, parents, and the nation's general citizenry will find the book of engaging interest. Professors in education departments should have the book in their professional libraries. Many different courses in education will find the book to be a valuable supplementary resource.

Chapter 1

Controversial Issues Being Encountered in Education at the Local Level

Part I

DEBATES THAT TEND TO INHIBIT SCHOOL SUCCESS

Primary Chapter Goal: To identify specific controversial issues in education at the local school level and the differences that exist among the citizenry for implementing them or retaining them in practice.

In the cases of religious practices, governmental legislation, labor relations, health care provisions, military actions, and other national activities, major differences of opinion regarding their proper place in America's priorities are commonly contested. However, none of the foregoing undertakings are any more controversial than those that are encountered in America's education programs. Just take a moment to think of a primary activity or program provision in America's school practices and procedures that does not carry with it some semblance of controversy or difference in its support.

For example, what about school busing, children's recess, homework, prayer in schools, student retention, evolution vs. intelligent design, and student grading? Differences in the practices of each of these activities loom large. In fact, it is not too unreasonable to believe that it is much easier to think of an educational provision or program in our schools that is controversial than to think of a program or activity that has a large majority of public agreement.

The importance of identifying education's controversial issues centers on the fact that such differences inhibit effective program operations and student achievement in several ways. The engagement of students in the learning process, the allocation of time needed for dealing with controversy, the maintenance of positive school/community relationships, the inhibition of gaining financial support, and the negative effects on personnel turnover in schools represent only a few of the negative outcomes resulting from educational controversy. Yet, controversy is with us and must be confronted if positive educational purposes are to be realized.

In this chapter, a selected number of the controversial issues in local school education are identified. In chapter 2, additional controversial issues at the local school are discussed as well. In both chapters, available empirical and basic research that serves to shed light on the positive and negative factors of the specific controversy is presented. Recommendations for resolving or reducing controversies will be discussed as fits the case. In chapter 3, emphasis is placed on those controversies that tend to be debated primarily at the state level. Similarly, chapter 4 will center on the major controversial topics that pervade the national scene.

The discussion in this chapter centers on many controversial issues/practices that are being encountered in contemporary schools. The number of controversial issues at the local school level seemingly is overwhelming. The discussions of the controversial issues are presented with no intention of viewing them in order of most relevant or important. It is not possible to include the entire number of contended issues in this book. This chapter's primary purpose is to identify objectively several primary controversial issues at hand and underscore the corresponding differences that are apparent in each debate.

The Homework Controversy

School homework has been a matter of special concern historically. The pro side tends to emphasize its benefits as a discipline and task completion activity whereby the con side underscores the child's need for relaxation and the child's time for increasing needs and skills in socialization. In regard to parental relations, those who favor homework cite its value in being able to see what children are learning in school and thus are more informed about ways to help them.

On the other hand, those who call for less or no homework for their children tend to emphasize the conflicts that result from pressure by parents to "do your homework," the outcomes of cheating, and as a "heavy hangs over thy head" activity. That is, it becomes a penalty in that the child has to do the homework before he or she can have fun doing things of his or her personal interest.

Homework practices today vary from policies of absolutely no homework to the "let's get tough position." Some persons contend that student achievement serves as an additional learning activity for time lost in the diversions at school that have negative effects on student learning. It makes up for the time lost.

The literature reports the opinions of various individuals who have their own ideas about how to resolve the homework debate. Such examples include the lessening of time required for homework assignments, including reducing the time factor for students in the primary grades and increasing it as the student moves into middle and high school.

Although such arrangements might serve to lessen the homework debate, nevertheless, homework assignments would continue and so would the debate. Home schooling, a practice that has increased over the years, is another example set forth to support the pro side of the homework debate. That is, some contend that home schooling has proven satisfactory for hundreds of students and is growing as an online activity. Thus, homework should provide an extended learning practice for others as well. Other pro and con arguments are as follows:

Student Homework: Other Often-Stated Pros

- Learning should be continued at home, not just in school. Independent learning is essential for continued success in adult life.
- Homework should be viewed and practiced as an extension of school work. Students just continue to work on school assignments at home rather than being in their seats in the classroom.
- Personal development is commonly viewed as self-improvement. Homework should be considered as self-improvement. It can be viewed as continued learning that is often stated in messages at graduation ceremonies: "Continue to Learn!"

Student Homework: Often-Stated Cons

- Homework has been associated with a number of detrimental health effects, including stress levels and frustration.
- It is best to do activities that foster student success and family relations: Have dinner together at home, read and play games in the home and outside, get the student to bed at a reasonable time.
- If homework were a prescription drug, it should be recalled!
- Schooling continues to place new pressures on students. Academic requirements and pressures to learn have required the "workday" of students to be far beyond the school day. After school, activities for students have pushed the school day to hours similar to those of adults. Adding homework to the student's day only results in added pressure.
- Homework deprives the students of having a fair chance to foster their health. Because of late hours of study, there is no time to relax and enjoy

life or to be sufficiently rested for the next day's learning activities and good health practices are inhibited.
- After excessive homework at night, family relations commonly are set aside.
Togetherness as a family and time with friends are sacrificed.
- Homework for whom? Who really does the homework? The student? The parents? A brother or sister? A friend?

The Controversial Issue of the Inclusive School

The courts have ruled that every student, including students with special needs, is eligible for placement in the least restrictive school environment. This ruling means that a special needs student can be placed in the normal classrooms with all other students or, if necessary, in special classrooms that can attend to the student' needs more effectively. As a result, the majority of classroom teachers say that they would rather not have these students in their classroom.

That is, the teacher does not always have the training that is necessary to deal with the wide variety of disabilities that are present with special needs students. In addition, there is some contention that the special needs of students "take time away" from other students in the classroom. On the other side of the debate, many persons contend that placing students in the regular classroom is not only their right but is best for them and for other students for the development of social skills, relationships, and cooperation that are encountered in life's work.

In a report by Debate.org (2018) titled *Should Education Students Be Mainstreamed?* The percentage of the study population that said "yes" was 37 percent, and 63 percent said "no." In the following section, specific thoughts by those persons who answered "yes" and "no" are noted. These responses serve to underscore the primary reasons for the mainstreaming debate.

Those persons in favor of mainstreaming special education students state that:

- Mainstreaming helps the special education student succeed more . . . it can help them gain social skills.
- Just because they're special needs doesn't mean they can't interact well with or learn with other people . . . [they] learn how to interact with other people and react to situations. . . . They can learn in a normal classroom environment if they are given a chance . . .
- Yes, yes yes . . . having them mainstream with regular kids helps them gain friends and boosts their confidence.

- Yes, if the child can even halfway keep up with their typical peers then why should they be denied the opportunity to try? Many cases of special needs improve greatly when they are able to see good examples of behavior and communication modeled by their peers.
- Yes, special needs children should be mainstreamed because it improves academics, social skills, and self-esteem.
- Without these students coming into a normal school, they might never get the knowledge and teaching they need to be successful in life.
- Mainstreaming gives the special education student a better chance at success . . . once they get to the point where they need it is the best thing you can do to help them.

The persons not in favor of mainstreaming of special education students state that:

- Their rights are not more important than those of normal children. Mainstreaming is expensive and it slows down the general population of a classroom.
- Mainstreaming is not usually the best choice. Most children with special needs do much better in a self-contained atmosphere. It is highly stressful for the student, teacher, and peers.
- Children with intellectual impairments have very different educational needs as compared to other students. . . . To have them struggling in a classroom so that they are with their peers will not benefit them in the future.
- No, special education students should not be mainstreamed. As suggested in the name, these students require special attention and have special needs. It also takes a certain trained professional to work with these students to get the most out of them at their pace. Not only would mainstreaming these students increase the difficulty of their learning, it would also deter the pace at which other students can be taught to allow the special students to keep up.
- Special education students need special assistance. While the idea of introducing special education students into a regular student environment may have noble intentions, it is not practical and in fact detrimental to both special and regular students.
- Mainstreaming benefits no one. The child being mainstreamed into a regular ed classroom needs way more one-on-one time than the teacher can provide, given that twenty = five students also need attention.

The foregoing statements give some reasons that the student inclusion debate continues. Experience in relation to the mainstreaming practices has provided some improvements that are leading to better solutions. The courts have ruled on the matter of student placement. In one case, the parent submitted an official complaint regarding her son's placement in a particular class with special needs students. She argued that she wanted her son placed in a more advanced and challenging classroom. The court ruled that the student's placement was appropriate in this case. The son was making academic progress in his present placement and that was all that was needed to meet the most effective placement ruling.

The Controversy of Sex Education Curricula in Schools

Attempts to establish the most serious controversial topics in local school education would likely be an exercise in futility. But, in most cases, the controversies related to sex education in schools would be near or at the top of the debate list. Some reports have indicated that 90 percent of the students' parents want sex education in the school curriculum but what information should be included and at what age it should be addressed are a big part of the debate. In instances where sex education has already been introduced in the schools' programs, parents commonly complain about what actually is being taught. In other cases, teachers contend that they were not consulted as to the sex ed curriculum or the age appropriateness for the topics being presented.

We note at the outset of this discussion that it is difficult to address and explain the debate relative to sex education in schools without using the terms associated with the topic. The sex ed terms reportedly listed on a poster of one middle school would raise the eyebrows of most readers. Adults would know and understand these terms, but younger children and youth might not. Some readers would view them as being vulgar.

In regard to the sex education debate, while one contingency favors the teaching of abstinence, others contend that high percentage of students already are engaged in sexual activities and that too many students are confronted with sexually transmitted diseases and unplanned pregnancies. Mandated standards for curricular topics tend to be overlooked by both parents and students. When local control of the sex education curriculum is promoted by state agencies and other groups, schools are accused of not paying attention to the set standards.

The topics of abortion, use of condoms, birth control pills, and other pregnancy control methods receive major criticisms from the proponents of abstinence. The contention is that these "protections" serve only to encourage engagement in sexual activities. The extent of the "problem" is exemplified by the various reports pertaining to the extent of sex activity among school students. For example, one report stated that one in four students have sex-related diseases. Teenage pregnancies and abortion statistics on the part of young persons are problematic as well.

Parents and others complain that publications on abortion are distributed in schools and that contemporary television promotes sex in its movies, programs, and advertisements. One source recommended that sex education be introduced in kindergarten, noting that the earlier sex education is initiated in the schools the better the outcomes. Others contend that sex education in the schools takes the responsibility away from parents. That is, it is best to leave the topic of sex education to appropriate sources outside the school. Others argue that these outside sources are commonly the students themselves. Thus, misinformation and lack of abstinence are the result.

A poster placed on a middle school's wall was shown in a photo on the web with the source being Fox News. Its title stated, "How do people express their sexual feelings?" Its listing of the sex education topics in the school's program would shock most readers. A resolution for the curriculum for sex education has to come about by an appropriate, effective education program, but what is appropriate and what program would be effective remain as the primary issues of debate.

Our recommendation would be for the parents, teachers, students, and administrators of each school to focus on the topic of sex education and attempt to arrive at a best solution for implementing a program of sex education within the school program. In some cases, site-based councils have been established for every school in the school district. In such cases, these councils could work toward an agreed-upon topical program for sex education in the school.

Such groups should keep an open-door policy as to their purpose and desired outcomes. Input from parents and others within the community should be sought. Such groups should not be secretive about what progress has been made and what input has been received from other sources in the community. The final program decision should not be a big surprise to the community members. After all, the final program instruction should reflect what has been gathered from community members along the way. At this point and time, what are your opinions/thoughts on the sex education debate? Is sex education a responsibility of the school? Why? Why not?

The Payment of Teachers; the Single Salary Schedule

The debate related to the use of the single salary model for paying teachers runs directly into the topic of performance pay. Nevertheless, we discuss the single salary schedule, that has been in operation in the large majority of school districts since the early 1950s, in terms of its pro and con contentions. As is commonly known, the single salary schedule is based on payments in relation to the teacher's years of experience and level of the educational degree held.

Historically, as the one-room school was taken over by increasing city populations, more schools with more teachers brought about problems of how to compensate teachers. The resolution was the concept of the single salary schedule that paid teachers equitably on the basis of their teaching experience and educational degree held. Beginning teachers were to be motivated to keep on learning and earn higher degrees and encouraged to remain in the school by receiving a step-up in pay with each year of teaching. The single salary schedule became so popular that by the early 1950s, virtually 97 percent of the nation's schools had adopted it as a method for teacher compensation.

The pros of single salary teacher compensation are as follows:

- Its simplicity. It is straightforward and easy to administer.
- It avoids favoritism and bias in compensating teachers fairly.
- It avoids the difficult task of trying to measure teacher production.
- It eliminates discrimination and bias in terms of age, gender, race, and ethnicity.
- It is easily managed and serves to project budget figures for the future.
- It is objective by paying on the teacher's experience and level of training (degree).
- It has proved its effectiveness for approximately seven decades.
- It encourages teachers to continue their training by giving credit for additional college credits.
- It creates cooperation among teachers rather than competition.
- Teaching is not a business and other compensation methods create competition rather than cooperation.

The cons of single salary teacher compensation are as follows:

- The single salary schedule does not recognize effective classroom performance. All teachers with the same level of experience and degree are paid the same regardless of their teaching results. It simply does not recognize effective teaching.
- It does not serve to attract or retain high-quality teachers. New compensation methods must be implemented to meet contemporary school program needs.
- A mediocre teacher receives the same pay as a high-quality teacher if both have the same educational degree and teaching degree.
- It does not hold teachers accountable for their teaching performance.

- New alternatives such as measuring their teaching effectiveness are now available.
- Some research shows that experience and degree bear little consistent relationships to student performance (Hanushek, 2003).
- It does not permit the school to attract high-quality personnel in general and inhibits the ability to attract and hire teachers in the higher academic subjects where competition is a serious concern.
- The cliché that "individuals enter teaching just because they love kids and compensation is not of great concern" is flawed. Innovative organizations base compensation on effective performance, and the single salary schedule does nothing to promote this outcome.
- It works against improvements in education programs.
- It assumes that teachers with more experience are more effective; empirical evidence has shown that this is not true.

Looking toward Better Solutions for School Funding

During the past twenty-five years, views related to how teachers should be compensated have changed. The new emphasis for compensation is based on teaching performance. Performance commonly is based on teacher evaluations and related student academic performance. There is evidence that many school districts have discontinued the use of the single salary system. Compensation programs that serve to reward effective teaching performance and to attract the interest of more persons toward a career in education are being implemented. When teacher compensation is linked to student test scores, however, teachers' organizations set forth a strong opposition.

The National Teachers Association, state agencies, and local school boards have implemented new compensation programs and discarded the years of experience plus earned degree methods as the bases for compensating teachers. We keep in mind that there are many hands involved in the matter of teacher compensation. First and foremost, perhaps, are the taxpayers themselves. Just as long as schools are funded by local and state taxes, politics will continue to play a large part in school funding.

The National Education Association, American School Boards Association, American Federation of Teachers, state legislatures, foundations, and federal agencies always have their say regarding financial support for education and, in some cases, determine how teaching performance might be rewarded. However, concepts of compensating teachers based on the performance of either teachers or students receive unfavorable responses, so the single salary schedule tends to remain in practice but not without recommendations for major improvements.

Recently, the South Carolina Education Association (SCEA, 2017) drafted a comprehensive statement of recommendation for improving the teacher salary schedule. In brief, two primary recommendations were as follows: (1) The state of South Carolina should increase the state's minimum salary schedule to raise the compensation floor for school districts, and (2) the state should provide support to school districts to restructure salary schedules to reduce the number of steps and enhance educators' career earnings.

Recommendations included the belief that teachers should be able to reach the maximum rate of compensation within ten years; a strong single salary schedule is based on the fewest possible steps/increments from entry level to the maximum rate of compensation. The foregoing South Carolina salary recommendations reportedly would serve the school district by offering competitive starting rates, serving as an effective recruitment and retention tool, reinforcing long-term relationships, and putting more spending power into the local economy.

The Educational Controversy of Student Discrimination, Including School Busing for Integration Purposes

Historically, student integration in schools has been one of the leading topics of controversy and debate within education. Although the record shows that considerable progress has been made in this crucial area, many groups and individuals insist that the problem has not yet been resolved. Integration in itself has been a leading topic of controversy historically. Great strides have been accomplished in this regard with the passing of integration legislation by the Supreme Court of the United States.

Among the notable civil rights legislation in the United States was the *Brown v. Board of Education* (341K7 U.S. 483,1952) (Topeka, Kansas), Civil Rights and Segregation. Although there was a white school just across the street from Linda Brown's home, she had to walk five miles to attend her school for blacks. The head of the National Association for the Advancement of Colored People, Thurston Marshall, took the case to the court, claiming that segregation laws violated the Fourteenth Amendment to the U.S. Constitution. Students were to receive equal treatment under the law. The state argued that the *Plessy v. Ferguson* case had settled this question and that separate but equal was being practiced. The court under Justice Earl Warren ruled in favor of the Brown family, and the initiation of integration was installed as the legal practice in America (Norton, 2016).

The matter of busing white school children into black neighborhoods to achieve desegregation came to the front as somewhat a different controversy. Its purpose, of course, was to bring more of a racial balance to school populations. This practice, according to Arthur Weinstein (2012, April 3), caused a myriad of problems exemplified by the cost of the busing that took funds from budgets that could be used to support school operations and teachers' salaries. Long rides on a bus for young students each day and problems related to busing and school boundaries were additionally contested. As would be understood, there was a divide in busing support with parents who had a successful local school and did not favor busing to some other site and parents who lived near a failing school and were somewhat favorable to the busing of their child to a more favorable school environment. The outcome? More controversy.

The Controversy over Cutting Curricular Offerings and School Activities Such as Recess

Decisions on the part of school boards to cut certain subjects from the curriculum and school activities such as the elimination of kindergarten, cutting recess for children, discontinuing fine arts offerings in music and art, de-emphasizing civics, reducing athletic activities, cutting afterschool activities, reducing the school time per day, or reducing the school attendance program from five days to four days each week have brought disgust and controversy to schools in many districts nationally. These cuts, of course, represent the insufficient financial support for education that has been in conflict historically.

Major differences in school districts' abilities to fund education remain present in the nation today. Reports indicate that the ability to fund education ranges on a ratio from 6 to 1. That is, the "richest" states, property-wise, are six times more able to fund education via property tax values than the poorest states in the Union. Measures to reach equity in this regard have been implemented but have not resolved the discrepancies to date.

Recess for children has come into the controversy arena among the nation's school districts. The controversy centers on the benefits of cutting recess for gaining more academic time for students to learn. However, those who support the continuation of recess for children underscore the fact that it is essential for fostering a learning attitude on the part of children and establishing a positive climate for learning. One report estimated that some schools have reduced the time to play by 40 percent. The various pro and con contentions in relation to children's recess are as follows:

Selected Pros for Retaining Recess

- First and foremost, recess promotes social and instructional learning for children. It serves to teach cooperation, leadership, and followership that are under adult supervision vs. adult direction.

- It is most helpful in helping children to learn the ways that conflicts are best resolved. In addition, playing the games at recess serves toward the releasing of tension and the reduction of boredom that often occurs, and learning about conflict resolution, compromise, and cooperation looms important as well.
- Learning is fostered by work breaks that are spaced over time. Recess serves this important purpose. It confronts the factors of participation and communication that are important for the development of a positive classroom climate.
- Recess includes the important activity of exercise, and it can help prevent obesity.
- It has been shown that recess serves to improve school climate, increase the children's attention, reduce disruptive behavior, and increase the school's positive climate.
- Children need to have a culture of play that serves to foster self-control and conflict resolution.

Selected Cons against Retaining Recess

- Recess presents many legal liabilities related to injuries due to getting hit, falling, and jumping.
- Teachers are hired to teach in the classroom rather than to oversee the problems related to playing games on the playground. Getting qualified helpers to supervise playground activities is troublesome in that they are hard to find, unreliable, and questionably qualified.
- Recess simply takes away time from the more valuable academic time in the classroom. Taking time to line up, walk outside, organize for play, walk back to the school building, use the restroom, and settle back down in the classroom can waste 30 minutes, sometimes twice each day, or more of academic learning time.
- Playtime commonly consists of more time for arguments about the rules of the game than playing the game itself. Time is wasted for classroom learning.
- Bullying takes place most often on the playground. Recess encourages such negative behavior. The contention that recess fosters social innovations is flawed.
- Many children, especially girls, are left out of the "organized play" that is more fit for boys. Girls become watchers rather than participants.
- Recess encourages cliques that leave some children outside the activity.
- Open campus playgrounds are invitations to the dangers posed by sexual predators.
- In some cases, recess does not work favorably for special needs children.
- Recess is all too often accompanied by the negative performance of bullying.

Whenever a course is added or cut from the school's curriculum, the chances of controversy come to the floor. Previously, we discussed the controversial issue of sex education in schools. However, the push for additional course instruction in cursive writing, civics, foreign language, vocational education, mathematics, science, the fine arts, business practices, health, and other subjects is a common request faced by school districts nationally.

In other situations, pressure to cut programs in foreign language, sex education, vocational education, industrial arts, home economics and kindergarten, and others has been opposed by one group or another. In fact, reportedly, some school districts have cut their sports programs, while others seem to have spent large sums of money to improve their sports facilities, increase travel, and pay for additional coaches for both boys' and girls' sports. Those who criticize school sports point to various problems of concern.

For example, the criticizers point out that students are being conned into the belief that sports are another path to glory; academic knowledge is not the only path. Yet, for the large majority of the students who engage in sports, it is certainly not the path to glory. As one opponent stated, sports for school kids have a short shelf life. That is, a very small percentage of the students who participate in sports during high school actually go on to participate at the higher college level. Sports for these students end as a sedentary lifestyle watching the sport from a seat in a stadium or on the couch at home. As a reader of this book, which side, pro or con, do you take on the matter of sports in high school?

The Controversy of Student Health

Health in relation to medical care, at this point and time, is near or at the top of major concerns of American citizens. Just like almost every national issue and problem, health has been placed on the agenda of school programs nationally. In regard to the health problems facing children and youth, the citizenry tends to look to the schools for dealing with the problems directly.

School programs historically have been concerned with student health. In the early 1930s, for example, underweight children were offered the "milk and graham cracker" nutrition program to be taken mid-morning at school each day. During these Depression days, these programs were costing parents 15 cents per week or 60 cents each month that some families could not afford. A school nurse was commonly available at least once a month to rule on students with minor health problems, perform vision tests, and give a hearing test for each child by whispering to them from 20 feet away.

In modern times, most all schools have special breakfast and lunch provisions for all or certain children and youth. Nursing care has been improved over the years, and special attention to children with special needs has grown by leaps and bounds. (Norton, Kelly, & Battle, 2012) listed 22 student disabilities and 12 student special services that most schools contend with today. Such services extend from those addressing speech and language pathologies to psychological services, physical and orthopedic therapies, medical services for diagnostic purposes, education for the mentally retarded, the autistic and those with learning disabilities, programs for students with vision or hearing impairments, serious emotional problems, or brain injury, and on and on (Norton, Kelly, & Battle, 2012).

The controversy? Most persons would agree that the work of the school in relation to student health is to be commended. Yet, the nature of many health conditions and the training to deal with them in a school environment are in question. There is no question that the courts have ruled the rights of special students to be placed in the best position for their successful learning, including the regular classroom with all other students. This provision was discussed previously in the section on the inclusive school. Empirical evidence suggests that special education programs and activities consume on average 30 percent of the school principal's total work time (Norton, Kelly, & Battle, 2012).

Although most all persons are sensitive to the needs of children with special needs, should the schools be held accountable for dealing with the overwhelming issues/problems surrounding the matter and still be held accountable for meeting the academic requirements of the school in terms of student achievement? There has been some talk of having the schools test some medications. Such talk, of course, causes much concern on the part of parents and other citizens. Should the priorities of school personnel be on teaching and learning specifically or be responsible for the health and learning success of children and youth? The contemporary answer appears to be both.

A somewhat different issue in this area centers on the expanding "demands" of parents to expect the schools to take care of their child's problems. Behavior, absenteeism, discipline, apathy, and disobedience are children's problems that are generally expected to be taken care by the parents in the home. Yet, principals and teachers report that it is common for parents to expect the school to take care of these discretions. The circumstance whereby both parents are working or the child is living with a single parent increases the problems related to this issue. To what extent is the school expected to take care of these kinds of special needs? School personnel most often say that these behaviors are the responsibility of parents. In turn, parents ask about what the school is doing to resolve these problems.

Once again, the partial problems are related to this question and the opinion of the large majority of teacher personnel is that they are not prepared and should not be held accountable for special needs children in their classrooms. This response is not one of disrespect or indifference; rather the majority of teachers contend that special needs children do not do their best in the regular classroom and such inclusion is unfair to them and other students academically.

The Controversy of Online Education in K–12 Schools

Online education is one of the fastest-growing trends in education technology. According to the U.S. Department of Education, more than 1 million K–12 students took online courses as early as 2007–2008. Nevertheless, online education is one of the most contentious programs today. We begin by considering why there is a high level of criticism of the online education activities.

The Cons of Online Education Programs for K–12 Students

- Online education is looked upon as a way to cut school costs. Cutting costs are being used to the detriment of student learning.
- There is a complete lack of research on the efficacy of online learning for K–12 students. Educationally, this is a serious oversight on the part of a professional organization.
- Online education is being used to supplant traditional classroom instruction. It trades teachers for technology.
- Online education is a scam job to push online learning so that companies can reap the rewards from the taxpayers.
- Online courses are too easy and used as a means to increase graduation rates without accompanying academic results.
- Unsupervised online education increases the use of plagiarism and does not give necessary consideration to individual student learning styles.
- Online learning simply gives access to more screen-time that leads to additional unhealthy and sedentary lifestyles.
- No studies have been found or controlled quasi-experimental studies completed to compare the effects of online education to show that it is better than face-to-face education that takes place in the school classroom.
- There is limited interaction with the course instructor. Thus, relationships and continued professional contacts and communication are averted. Social interaction in a campus environment is greatly inhibited. Professional relationships with the instructor and institution of record are greatly reduced.
- The claim of online education as being a self-directed activity is easily erased. It is too easy to procrastinate and self-direction is not always used.
- There is a stigma or misconception that online is easier, but this is not always the case. There is always the question of who is really doing the work.
- Technology requirements and access to computers are technical problems that must be encountered in online education. Such problems being encountered commonly turn off the student's engagement in the online method.

- Trouble trying to transfer the credit of an online course to a traditional school presents some problems. This matter is seldom clarified before the student enrolls in the online course.
- Online students have found themselves involved in a scam and involved with a credit or degree mill operation. Some online programs advertise that the learner can even list the name of their graduation diploma/degree themselves on the program application.
- The online education method is used by the individual with the potential of having many necessary and unnecessary distractions at home. There are ongoing interruptions with the family and other sources that inhibit the student's focus.
- Giving parents the primary control/responsibility for controlling the child's education carries with it a number of problems. In fact, are parents really prepared to determine and direct the academic education of children? Consider the actual involvement of a large proportion of parents that do not get involved in their child's education now. Won't most children be in control of what they want to do educationally rather than what they need to do to be prepared for their life ahead?

Perhaps the foregoing cons are overly stated or are criticisms that might not be objective and factual. Nevertheless, they do represent entries into the list of criticisms of K–12 online education programs that have been voiced on the topic.

On the other hand, supporters of online education set forth statements that follow on the online education concept:

The Pros of Online Education Programs for K–12 Students

The positive establishment of online education programs in K–12 school programs was previously noted. Online education has made its way into public school programs as well as into major higher education programs nationally. The success of these programs and the factors for their success are expressed in the following list of pro comments.

- Online education courses are especially convenient in terms of flexibility and availability. Such courses enable many students to complete school work that otherwise might be most difficult or impossible for them to complete.
- Availability is demonstrated by the fact that more and more online school programs are open for the learner's convenience. Access to the program is 24/7.

- Location and availability are further demonstrated by the fact that online programs are conveniently located and available among the states and within the counties. You can pursue online education from wherever you are located, including service in the military.
- Online courses have the convenient characteristic of zero commuting. Costs for travel are reduced and one's time is saved.
- Online education is based on the quality of self-direction. The learner can work at his or her own pace. Self-development has been identified as the best concept for personal improvement; online education provides this opportunity.
- The makeup of online courses is most comprehensive. More choices are available to meet the learner's personal needs and interests.
- The learner is able to take many courses that are not necessarily available in the local school program.
- Online education provides a ready program for making up classes that one might have not completed previously or possibly failed.
- Online education serves to meet the problem of teacher shortages and help retain teachers. Empirical evidence has demonstrated that online education can eliminate teaching jobs that helps to resolve the teacher shortage.
- A positive factor of online education is that it is one way to cut school costs. The funding of school programs is high on the list of education's major issues and problems.
- Online education programs can provide a greater variety of options for the learner by adding a greater selection of program electives.
- Online education permits some students to take advantage of advanced placement courses within the present school district or under the auspices of a local, county, or state higher education facility.
- Students who participate in the online education programs are among the millions of the nation's students who are doing the same. Online education is showing its potential every year as being the most innovative method for increasing learning opportunities for the nation's K–12 students.
- A strong support factor of online K–12 education rests in the fact that it gives the parents of the child the primary control of the child's education.
- Education authorities historically have voiced the importance of having education program activities based on the individual student's primary interests and needs. Aren't the parents of the children and the children themselves at the secondary school levels in the best position to know about their interests in learning?
- Online education is great for those with family responsibilities.

The future of online K–12 education seemingly will continue to grow in a dramatic fashion. As is commonly the case, however, no valid and reliable research has been devoted to the topic. Will research on the topic in the near future give us a much better idea as to the efficacy of online learning? Or will online learning continue to expand due to its probability of being a formative money-maker for financial investors?

Major differences in school district's ability to fund education remain present in the nation today. Reports indicate that the ability to fund education ranges on a ratio from 6 to 1. That is, the "richest" states, property-wise, are six times more able to fund education via property tax values than the poorest states in the Union. Measures to reach equity in this regard have been implemented but have not resolved the discrepancies to date. Additional thoughts on these matters are discussed in other chapters of the book.

The Controversial Issue of Excessive Administrative Personnel in School Operations

The final controversial issue in K–12 education to be discussed in this chapter centers on the number of administrative personnel who are being hired to operate the district's schools today. In the early 1930s, the elementary school was managed primarily by a single teacher/administrator who served as a classroom teacher and as the school's secretary and principal as well. In most cases, teaching was the individual's primary interest. It is true that many elementary schools were viewed as neighborhood schools in that each school had one class of 20–30 students at each of the seven grade levels K–6, and were often relatively close to one another, and located on one to two acre lots.

As the nation's population increased dramatically and city schools became crowded with students, larger schools were established and new program services were initiated. School principals, assistant principals, support staff personnel, custodial personnel, and nurses were among the personnel hired at the elementary school level. At the junior high and high schools, support staff increased considerably; school counselors, truancy personnel, assistant principals, department chairs, security personnel, and facility managers were found in many schools.

However, today the school district's central administrative office building commonly includes personnel for the supervision of curriculum and staff development, student testing and assessment, school board–related functions, state and federal relations, legal services, human resources services, supervision of maintenance and facilities, food service operations, vocational and industrial arts curriculum, athletic program management, special education management services, school district communication and public relations office, business management services, and other support services.

Those groups and individuals who question the need for improved school funding most often point to the need to reduce the administrative management numbers in the school and to reorganize the number of separate school districts into one efficient entity. Although many states have set forth school district reorganization legislation, many others have not. The idea of keeping their schools close to home is reflected in the voices of those citizens who disfavor school district reorganization.

The Controversy of the Self-Contained Classroom vs. the Open Classroom Concepts

The controversy over the self-contained classroom vs. the open classroom concept was not considered for inclusion in this chapter until we learned that the concept is not dead but once again is being promoted in a state university's teacher preparation program. The term used for implementing the open classroom concept is *reimagining education*. The open classroom concept received major attention in the 1970s but began to fade in most school districts that had given it a try. At that time, the open classroom concept was piloted in 13 of the 27 elementary schools in one Nebraska school district. It soon faded primarily due to the fact that teachers in the pilot schools had major difficulties trying to set aside the same instructional practices that they had used previously in the self-contained classroom.

The open classroom concept was initiated in another large elementary school district in Arizona several years ago. It too was discarded soon thereafter. What are some of the support views of the open classroom concept, and what are some of the non-support views? The following section sets forth several of these thoughts in the form of pros and cons.

Examples of Pro Views in Support of the Open Classroom

- The open classroom concept allows the learners to move around and explore their own learning needs and interests. It fosters student-centered learning.
- The open classroom concept provides an opportunity for the student to develop and utilize his or her own creative talents that the traditional classroom does not provide.
- The open classroom does lead to the actual student collaboration that has been missing in the traditional classrooms.
- The open classroom makes it possible for teachers to know what's going on around them and to connect with others' activities.
- The teacher is able to pick up ideas and techniques from other teachers within their vicinity.
- The teacher learns to adjust to the changes that occur in the open classroom. They learn to adjust to the changes, including the noise that open classrooms commonly have due to the business of the students' activities.

- Open sessions with parents are more successful; meeting in the regular classroom with the door closed places certain inhibitors on the conversation.
- It is easy for a teacher to move to a different group of students and serve instructionally. Cooperative teaching is made more possible.
- Although the open classroom is different at first, one learns to adjust and to appreciate the new relationships that take place.

Examples of the Con Views in Opposition to the Open Classroom

- The open classroom is too loud, too distracting. Teachers tend to hate it!
- The open classroom can be very loud. You don't feel free to make a lot of noise with certain activities.
- Teachers feel spied upon.
- The open classroom can be disruptive.
- Collaboration can also be an obstruction when it comes to students' individual tasks.
- One has to raise his or her voice in order to be heard.
- There is a lack of reliable and valid research behind the idea.
- The noise factor is the number-one problem when trying to get students to focus on what the teacher is saying.
- Teachers tend to retain the closed-door classroom methods. Walls are created anyway. Bulletin boards are on wheels, crates are stacked up, metal cabinets serve as dividers, bookshelves are placed to enclose a group, hangers are used to drape things down to enclosure a class of students.

Some credit is given to the original concept of the open classroom. There is some evidence that the open classroom concept has left certain ideas for improving the instruction in the traditional classrooms. Student collaboration activities, student-centered learning, cooperative teaching strategies, and student exploration are among those concepts that might serve to improve student engagement in the regular classroom environment. In any case, one never knows if or when a former idea or practice might rise to the front once again.

History has demonstrated that a "discarded" concept in education has a tendency to come and go. One example is that of student physical fitness that was emphasized during the presidential term of John F. Kennedy. Others are exemplified by the emphasis on vocational education, the new mathematics, teaching phonics, cursive writing, and emphasizing civics.

The Controversial Topic of Cursive Writing

Many schools nationally have either discontinued or dropped the teaching of cursive writing in the elementary grades. Cursive writing is the type of penmanship in which some characters are written joined together in a flowing manner. The cursive method has been taught at the elementary school level historically generally for making writing faster.

The term *cursive* derives from the eighteenth-century Italian *corsivo* and Medieval Latin *cursivus*, which literally means "running." The Latin derivation is *currera* meaning "to run" or "hasten" (Wikipedia, 2018b). The general controversy centers on the need for students to be efficient in typing in order to be able to use the computer for communication and searching for information and the belief that cursive writing is no longer needed in contemporary practices. The key pro argument against the dropping of cursive writing in the school centers on research reports that it can have significant benefits for brain development. Of course, there are various pros and cons regarding the teaching of cursive writing in schools, and these differences are noted in the following section.

Argued Pros for Retaining Cursive Writing in School Curriculums

- Certain research results have revealed that cursive writing has many advantages over typing on a keyboard.
- The individual's cursive writing style is a personal thing that is maintained throughout one's life.
- Cursive writing serves to benefit the child's brain development according to several authorities. This development is not present when using the keyboard.
- Some persons have found that knowing cursive writing also serves in a positive way in learning other second languages.
- It isn't a matter of either learn cursive writing or not. A student who is skilled in cursive writing can, like millions of other individuals, become skilled with typing skills as well.
- When a student is reading a book at home or in a classroom, taking notes in cursive writing is relatively easy. Having to use a typing keyboard does present some problems.
- Students are more literate if they can read and write cursive, and it allows them to communicate with older people and family members.
- Students can sign their names, which is a standard requirement during life.
- Students can take notes faster in school and in college.
- The most important documents are written in cursive (e.g., U.S. Constitution and Declaration of Independence).
- If the student does not learn cursive writing skills, he or she will miss many enjoyments in life such as the reading of some historical documents, letters received in cursive writing, various messages left or sent to him or her in cursive, and certain historical documents left in the family over the years.

- It is good for one's brain according to many cursive writing specialists.
- Reportedly, it is helpful to students with dyslexia.
- It unlocks a wealth of historical knowledge.
- Cursive hand writing is a form of creativity.
- States like Tennessee, Louisiana, and California have made cursive writing a state standard.

Argued Cons against Retaining Cursive Writing in School Curriculums

- Cursive writing has gone way of the typewriter, abacus, and slide rule.
- It takes time away from core subjects.
- It is not valued as it once was.
- Poor penmanship is always in evidence, and this causes problems.
- Reportedly, $95 million in tax funds are not delivered correctly because of unreadable tax returns forms.
- Creative writing is simply no longer important.
- One can read and do a lot of things without knowing cursive writing.
- Cursive writing is not required in Common Core Standards.
- One survey revealed that handwriting teachers rarely use it themselves.

As noted in the pro statements favoring cursive writing, some states have set forth a requirement to continue cursive writing in the schools, while others have dropped it from the curriculum. In the next chapter of the book, we address the available research that pertains to several of the controversies discussed in chapters 1 and 2. The debate on cursive writing will be included in this research report. The research results for this subject are not only interesting but also somewhat amazing. You will find it to be of great interest.

History has demonstrated that a "discarded" concept in education has a tendency to come and go. One example is that of student physical fitness that was emphasized during the presidential administration of John F. Kennedy. Others are exemplified by the emphasis on vocational education, the new mathematics, teaching phonics, cursive writing, and civics. Can you think of others?

Looking to Chapters That Follow

This chapter has included several of the leading controversial issues facing America's school personnel and local school communities. Other chapters return to these issues to discuss important research that has been centered on some of them and will also give attention to other debates that are primarily internal to the schools and those that have been brought about by groups and agencies external to local school districts. Student grading reports, teacher assessment and evaluation, student rights, teachers' workload, technology utilization, going green, standardized testing, bilingual education, guns in school, student dress, cursive writing, social media, cyber-bullying, four-day school week, and others are examples of debates that are essentially internal debates.

Funding, teacher licensure, core curriculum, local control, vouchers, accountability, standardized testing, education standards, student rights, poverty, state/federal controls, court mandates, and others are examples of controversies that are external in nature. That is, these debates include people, groups, agencies, and governance mandates that are placed on schools with accompanying penalties for not complying. Several of these controversies are discussed in the chapters that follow.

Key Chapter Ideas and Recommendations

- Many school practices and programs receive criticism and debate regarding their place in the curricular program of children's school. Traditional programs of the school as well as new innovations are questioned and debated in school districts today.
- The importance for the school personnel to identify and work to resolve controversial issues rests on the fact that such differences tend to inhibit program operations and effective student achievement.
- The debate issues/problems facing schools are so prevalent that it is virtually impossible to deal with all of them satisfactorily.
- Rules and law vary such that it often becomes the result that you can do this but you can't do that. Such a debate is exemplified by the issue of prayer in schools.
- Various controversial matters have been ruled upon by the U.S. Supreme Court. One example of this action is the court's ruling on inclusiveness on the part of student placement.
- Research on various controversial issues is missing. In other cases, research is indeed available but is ignored in education. One such example is that of research on student retention in grade.
- Some controversies have a long history. That is, these debates have been present for many years without being resolved.
- Solutions to many educational debates are evasive and seemingly impossible to resolve.

- Solutions to the problems surrounding many controversial issues depend on valid and reliable research that seems to be absent in education generally.
- Controversial courses are subject to cultural changes and political demands. Program pressures for improved physical education programs in schools, increased attention to new mathematics methodology, improvements in vocational education, major improvements in the school's reading program, and others serve as examples.
- One of the primary problems facing education today is that of politics. Keeping education out of politics is a vacant cry today. As politics changes, and it always does, so do the thoughts about what should and should not be taught in our schools.
- Student failure does not inspire success nor does it serve to develop a realistic sense of one's own strengths and weaknesses.

Discussion Questions

1. This chapter presented several controversial topics being encountered in education today. Which of these debates have some relation to your school situation or a school for which you are most familiar? List two or three controversial issues that are present in your school or one for which you are most familiar.
2. In a school class related to social studies or other discussion groups, select two of the controversial practices/programs discussed in this chapter and divide members into teams of pro and con and hold an actual debate using the common debate procedures.
3. Ask your parents to identify several primary controversial issues that they encountered as a student in school. Make note of their responses and then compare your parents' list with the debated issues discussed in this chapter.
4. Assume that you have been asked to discuss the controversial issue of prayer in schools at a meeting of the parent-teacher association. Give thought to your five-minute presentation. What major points might you set forth?
5. Several primary controversial issues were presented in this chapter. These and additional debated topics will be discussed in other chapters of this book. Why do you believe there are so many controversial issues facing education today? Don't just give responses such as "people just don't agree on things anymore" or "there are too many troublemakers in the world today." Rather, try to derive at specific reasons that controversy tends to be ongoing historically.

Case Study: The Controversy surrounding Professional Development of Teacher Personnel

The Lafayette School District had just elected three new members to its seven-member school board. Each of the three new members had run on a platform of improving education in the Lafayette School District. Lafayette schools had 23 elementary schools, 3 middle schools, and 2 high schools. All but three of its elementary schools had received state scores of underperforming. All three of its middle schools had scores of underperforming, and one of its high schools had the same low rating.

Superintendent Torrval Johnson was well aware that the forthcoming school board agenda was going to center on the academic performance results. State testing centered primarily on the areas of reading, mathematics, science, and English language arts. As might be expected, administrators and teachers at the middle and secondary levels placed the blame of the low scoring on the fact that the elementary schools were not preparing their students sufficiently for the school work in the upper grades.

School principals were fast to support the effectiveness of their teacher personnel. Forty-five percent of the elementary and 55 percent of the middle and secondary teachers had master's degrees. However, school personnel included curriculum coordinators for elementary, junior high, and high school programs; vocational and industrial arts supervisors; music and orchestra coordinators; special education personnel administrators; business managers and related personnel; school facility administrators; professional librarians; guidance directors; instructional resources managers; athletic directors; public relations personnel; adult education services personnel; student lunch managers; one or two assistant school superintendents; and a school superintendent. Some reports have contended that the administrative staff in school districts now numbers 50 percent of the total school district's personnel.

The elementary school personnel expressed the view that the minority population had increased significantly during the past five years and many parents were not able to help their children with math and science. Reading help was especially troublesome. School board members were adamant in the belief that the teaching effectiveness was the primary requirement for successful learning by the student population. After all, other school districts with minority populations apparently were doing a better job of teaching since their test scores were far more positive. Thus, teacher improvement was foremost on the minds of school board members for ameliorating the current problem of low student achievement.

The school board approved a requirement for all teachers to acquire an additional 12 credit hours in the area of their teaching specialty within the next 12 months. Emphasis was placed on the recommendation to complete this work at the earliest possible time. Teachers who did not meet the requirement would not move ahead on the salary schedule.

Alfred Roeder, president of the local teachers' association, asked for a special meeting with the board. At the special meeting, Roeder contested the requirement of professional growth and indicated that it was a violation of the teachers' contracts. In addition, he stated that the low testing results could not be placed at the door of the school district's teachers. All Lafayette teachers held valid teaching certificates and were doing everything possible to meet the needs of the school district's diverse study body.

The teacher who accompanied Roeder to the special session, at one time, stood and commented, "Why don't you just leave us alone, we're professionals." Roeder closed his remarks by indicating that a teacher walkout could be the result of the school board's actions if not withdrawn. Approximately, one-half of the parents who attended the special session were in favor of the board's actions, another one-fourth was opposed to such actions, and the other one-fourth was undecided.

Discussion Questions

1. Your task is to assume the role of the Superintendent Johnson and set forth what you would do administratively at this point and time. Be specific by writing out a paragraph or two as to your administrative actions following the special meeting. What additional information might be especially helpful? What legal information might you collect? What groups or individuals might you meet or address?
2. It seems important that you meet with your school board with your thoughts and recommendations at this time. After all, a teachers' walkout just might be a most difficult situation for the school district to contend. Draft a statement that sets forth the key points that you will make at the school board session.

Case Study: HELP Requests Your Support

Hispanic Educational Leadership Program

May 1, 2019

Dale Royce, Principal
Whittier Middle School
Fairview, Lafayette 1235

Dear Mr. Royce:

As you are aware, nearly 40 percent of the Whittier Middle School students are Hispanic and reports are that only 12 percent of the teachers are Hispanic. The Hispanic Educational Leadership Program (HELP) has passed a resolution to request two changes for the forthcoming school year.

(1) Increase the percentage of Hispanic faculty in the school district proportionately to that of the Hispanic student enrollment, and
(2) Increase the program of bi-lingual education to accommodate all students in the school.

At this time, HELP requests your support in achieving these equity goals. May we receive your response at this time regarding your thoughts and your action plan for Whittier School relative to the aforementioned goals?

Sincerely,
Raul Gomez, Chairman

HELP
cc: Quentin Bogart, Supt. of Schools
Vera Sanchez, President of the School Board

Discussion Questions

1. Assume the role of Principal Royce and respond to the questions posed in the letter sent to you by Raul Gomez. Refrain from "stone walling" by giving general answers such as "I will think about this matter and return a response latter" or "This is a matter outside my jurisdiction." That is, give a professional response to this person's request.
2. Give consideration to the follow-up of this request in regard to a plan. Include your plan in the return letter to Mr. Gomez.

REFERENCES

Debate.org (2018). Should special education students be mainstreamed? https://www.debate.org/opinions/should/special-education-students-be-mainstreamed.

Hanushek, E. A. (2003). The failure of input-based schooling policies. *Economics Journal,* 113 (485), 64–98.

Norton, M. S., Kelly, L. K., & Battle, A. R. (2012). *The principal as student advocate: A guide for doing what's best for all students.* Larchmont, NY: Eye on Education.

Report Post (2012, April 22). *Should special education students be mainstreamed?* Debate.org. https://www.debate.org/opinions/should-special-education-students-be-mainstreamed.

Rider, K. (2014). *Supreme Court rulings on prayer in public schools: 5 best facts about historic cases.* West Palm Beach, FL. Newmax Media, Independent American.

SCEA (2017). *The SCEA teacher salary schedule recommendations.* Marcy Magid (Senior Policy Analyst. https://www.thescea.org/wpcontent/upload/2017/101/The-SCEA-Teacher-Salary-Schedule-Recommendations-R83117–1.pdf.

Weinstein, A. (2012, April 3). *5 most controversial issues in U.S. education.* https://listosaur.com/category/miscellaneous.

Chapter 2

Controversial Issues Being Encountered in Education at the Local Level

Part II

Primary Chapter Goal: To continue the discussion of the controversial issues that are being encountered at the local school level.

This chapter continues to focus on the major controversies being encountered by local school districts. It is clear, however, that the local schools are not alone in their efforts to resolve these matters. School prayer, for example, has been a primary problem for both state and national governance offices. Its importance has reached the U.S. Supreme Court. Other educational controversies include the matters of the teaching of evolution and creationism in the school's science curriculum, school busing as it pertains to racial integration, online education, and sex education. Each of these debates and others are discussed in this chapter.

The Controversial Issue of Prayer in School

We begin the discussion with the topic of prayer in schools, a topic that has caused great contention historically among the general citizenry in the United States. As stated by Weinstein (2012), "Don't expect any of these controversies to go away soon, as some have lingered for decades" (2).

An earlier Gallup Poll survey indicated that over three-fourths of the study population favored voluntary prayer in schools and would support an amendment to the U.S. Constitution that allowed such practices (Education. com, 2012). On one hand, prayer in schools is viewed as a positive factor in the development of moral guides for core beliefs about sin, creation, life after death, faith, heaven, and hell. On the other hand, parents and others are greatly concerned that prayer and other religious activities will impose upon the thinking of students and indoctrinate them in ways that are contrary to what they believe is true.

In considering the matter of prayers in school, it tends to become "yes, you can do this," and "no, you can't do that." Then again, what you can or cannot do might well depend on the state in which you live. The question seems to rest on the fact as to whether the school (teacher or others) is trying to indoctrinate the student into certain religious beliefs or if the student is "practicing" religion in his or her own way. It seems clear, however, that it is unconstitutional for the school to compose an official school prayer and encourage its recitation by students (*Engel v. Vitale*, 370 U.S. 421 [1962]).

A teacher is most likely to be OK in saying Merry Christmas to a colleague but is in violation if he or she wishes a Merry Christmas to all members of the class. You can put up a Christmas tree inside the school building, but it has to be removed so as not to infer a school "instructional" symbol. Silent prayer has been approved in many court challenges but remains alright if not forced on each and every student.

We conclude this introductory discussion of school prayer by noting the primary pros and cons related to several educational controversies. The notation begins by considering examples of the primary favorable pro points of view of prayer in schools.

Prayer in Schools: The Often-Stated Pros

- Prayer gives credibility to the concept of religious freedom that supports students' rights.
- The First Amendment to the Constitution has been misinterpreted in this regard. A simple prayer by students in a school certainly does not constitute the establishment of a religion.
- Prayer at anytime and anywhere has many benefits. Prayer in schools serves to provide a sense of positive moral behavior in schools and the community.
- Prayer in schools serves to support the moral values carried out in the home and within the school community. Thus, it centers on the basic needs of children and the essential behaviors expected of each individual.
- Prayer in schools serves to provide an expected way one must act morally and gives the student a foundation for determining his or her personal life choices.
- Since the courts have already ruled that students are allowed to pray in schools on a voluntary basis, it already is legalized as a practice of a student in a school.

Prayer in Schools: The Often-Stated Cons

- The First Amendment to the U.S. Constitution sets forth the requirement that the government shall not adopt laws that serve to establish a religion. Schools, as government agencies, are supported by public funds. Therefore, prayer in schools, that is sanctioned and led by school personnel, is in violation of establishing a religion.
- It has been emphasized historically that there must be a separation of church and state. Public schools are funded by taxes, and thus prayer in schools leads to nothing more than the establishment of a religion and therefore is unlawful.
- Praying in school differs according to the religious belief of the individual. Thus, beliefs tend to differ, and intolerance among students is a logical outcome. We need to remedy intolerance, not promote it.
- Schools are required to remain neutral on religious issues. Increasing diversity in the student population makes this position virtually impossible. Thus, prayer in schools is divisive rather than being a factor that enhances student positive behavior.
- Prayer in schools tends to interfere with the responsibilities of parents in their attempts to establish moral principles in the lives of their children. Prayer, therefore, is most effective when it is part of the child's life in his family home, not in the school.
- The court case of *Engel v. Vitale* makes it clear that a school cannot compose an official prayer and encourage its recitation by students.

Ridder (2014) cited several court rulings regarding the matter of prayer in public schools. In 1963, the U.S. Supreme Court ruled that teachers were not allowed to lead prayer or Bible readings even if the activity is optional. Teachers and students can pray in schools if the prayer is voluntary and does not give the impression that the school is organizing or directing it. In addition, teachers can participate in a voluntary manner but cannot give the impression that the school administration is organizing or directing it. Teachers can participate in a voluntary manner as long as it is clear that participation is not part of their official capacity as a teacher. It seems clear that the rulings leave some fine lines to be determined when any student/school prayer is practiced.

The Controversial Issue of Evolution, Creationism, and Intelligent Design Instruction

The issue of whether or not to teach evolution in schools as an alternative to creationism, and vice versa, is on the table of many schools. The Kansas Board of Education took a major policy step by voting to delete evolution from its new state science standards (Wikipedia, 2018). The U.S. Supreme

Court has ruled the teaching of creationism as a science in public schools to be unconstitutional, irrespective of how it might be purveyed in theological or religious instruction. In any case, the discussion of controversies related to the teaching of creationism and evolution in schools is difficult at best.

Nevertheless, we begin the discussion by defining terms and then noting the primary pros and cons in relation to the teaching of this subject in school. It is commonly known that the U.S. Constitution prohibits the teaching of religion in the nation's public schools. However, due to court rulings on the subject, some school programs are incorporating certain information on the science of life in the curriculum.

The Five Primary Positions for the Development of the World's Life Features

The term *evolution* refers to the concept/belief that all living things can be traced to the same microscopic organisms. Changes and mutilations over time take place with natural selection of the strongest species. *Creationism* centers on the Bible's version of life. God created the life forms on earth without using prior, extinct life forms to do so. *Intelligent design* centers on the belief that the world features and living things are best explained by an intelligent cause, not an undirected process such as natural selection. It is based on a "scientific process" of observation, hypothesizing, experimentation, and arriving at conclusions.

On one hand, *theistic evolution* is complementary to evolutionary creationism that regards God as compatible with modern scientific understanding about biological evolution: how scientific theory relates to religious beliefs. On the other hand, *atheistic evolution* is one of the origin-of-life views that is based on Darwinian evolution beliefs of natural selection and survival of the fittest.

This controversy in education has resulted in lawsuits across the country. As noted more than a decade ago by Allen (2006), the evolution versus intelligent design debate has focused on what students ought to know and should be tested. The debates as to the matters of school accountability and academic standards have resulted in states and local school boards wrangling over educational standards with concerns for cultural climate along with the factors of religious and political differences. The outcome of the national/state controversies, however, has been expecting the primary locales of those issues under debate—local schools—, to also be where those issues will play out and be resolved.

We close the discussion on the foregoing debate by noting the major pros and cons for having certain science information taught in the school classrooms. Check these contentions and think about which side of the issue you support at this time.

The Pro Positions for Teaching of Evolution, Creationism, and Intelligence Design

- Intelligent design is science supported by many scientists. Therefore, it is proper for schools to teach this science in their curricular program.
- There is more evidence to back up intelligence design and evolution; it seems more logical than believing in a heavenly being.
- Intelligent design has been endorsed by nearly 1,000 PhD scholars.
- Public schools already encourage students to engage in critical thinking. They already are studying other scientific theories, so intelligent design is a proper study for students.
- Both creationism and intelligent design should be taught; this is part of the purposes of teaching science.
- A few years ago, a district judge struck down a statement endorsing intelligence design as violating the separation of church and state.
- The teaching of critical theories is being promoted by school boards nationally. Why not evolution and intelligence design?
- No one can prove that God does not exist. So, creationism certainly can be the rationale for life on the world. Scientists can't explain some DNA mutations that do not coincide with evolution theory.

The Con Positions against the Teaching of Evolution, Creationism, and Intelligence Design

- Teaching these subjects violates the ruling of separation of church and state.
- Intelligence design is not a science; no credible scientific body supports the theory.
- Students should not be bullied into believing an agenda presented by the teacher, principal, or school district.
- Intelligence design is merely a religious content disguised as a science, but isn't supported by scientists.
- Students are not being taught to think like scientists.
- Students are not legally allowed to take part in religious debates. Creationism is such a religious belief.
- Courts have ruled as far back as 1987 (*Edwards v. Aguillard*) that creation cannot be taught alongside evolution in public schools.

In the past few years, some state legislative bodies have considered some form of debate surrounding the inclusion of intelligence design in the schools' science classes. Reportedly, the teaching of critical theories is being promoted by school boards nationally. One example was the critical-thinking exercise of discussing atheistic vs. theistic evolution. Purpose is centered on critical thinking rather than on the nature of the religious teaching.

Educationally, the key questions to be asked and considered include: Should the topics of evolution, intelligence design, and creationism have an instructional place in the science curriculum of a public school? Are these and related topics so disruptive that none of them should be part of an effectively administered school program? Or, does the exclusion of these subjects work against the important education purpose of over-controlling what is learned and inhibiting the factors of critical thinking and presenting only those subjects that the school board and instructional personnel want the students to learn at school? Isn't it possible, like sex education, that students will learn about them elsewhere?

The Controversy of Student Retention in Grades

An early article, by Norton (1983), carried the title "It's Time to Get Tough on Student Promotion, Or Is It?" The article asked the question as to whether the practice of "social promotion" of students via grades was causing the problem of the low academic standing of students in the United States. Shouldn't students be required to be retained in a grade in school if they were not really prepared to move to the next grade level? On the one hand, the pro side contends that promoting students to the next grade level, if they had not "mastered" the work required in the present grade, is flawed. That is, they contend that students should be required to repeat a grade if academic performance is below the standards.

Several arguments have been voiced by "get tough" proponents on retention who present the opinions that follow:

1. Retention ensures greater mastery of subject matter; that is, holding the pupil back provides a needed opportunity for success later in the later grades.
2. Retention, especially in the early grades, is one way to help pupils have adequate time to grow and mature, thereby increasing readiness and learning success.
3. Retention serves to reduce the range of abilities in classes and therefore places pupils closer to their "peers" in relation to learning.
4. Non-promotion serves as a motivational incentive to pupils; that is, the practice of pupil retention awakens the laggard and serves to remove pupil apathy. (Norton, 1983, 283)

Those groups and individuals who oppose student retention think otherwise. For example, anti-retention proponents set forth beliefs such as those that follow:

1. Retention does not improve student achievement. In fact, students who are allowed to move ahead to the next grade commonly learn more the next year than if they were retained in grade.
2. Retention in grade does not increase socialization or learning readiness. Retained students often show actual regression.

3. Non-promotion does not increase the homogeneity of groups. Non-promoted students tend to choose companions from grades higher than their own.
4. Non-promotion tends to foster discipline problems, is a negative influence on their self-concept, and might result in a negative way as to the retained student's self-image
5. Some studies have reported that students who are not retained, but allowed to move ahead with their peers, learn more in the next grade than if they were retained. (Norton, 1983, 283)

Determining the percentage of students withheld in grade each year is difficult.

Although retention figures are reported in many articles within the literature, the base information tends to differ from case to case. In many reports, the higher retention statistics reveal that the results included a large number of Hispanic students who "needed more instruction" in their present grades. Nevertheless, statistics reveal that of the estimated 50 million students in the nation's schools, 5 to 10 percent are retained in grade each year. This statistic indicates that a minimum of 2.5 million students are retained in grade annually.

In addition, empirical evidence has revealed that if a student is retained in grade even once, the possibility of being a school dropout is quite high. Contemporary calls for higher standards for pupils in schools often result in an increase in student retention. The point of concern in chapter 1, however, is the fact that student retention is still being practiced in school today and continues to be included in the arena of controversy in education. Those groups that oppose student retention argue that it places a "black mark" on the student that can never be removed. Those groups that favor retention argue that it places the student at his success level and increases his or her ability to learn. In brief, virtually all studies of student retention in grades have concluded that retention has no merit academically.

In view of the many research studies that find that student retention is not a positive practice, we support the policy for non-retention. In fact, we found no research that indicated that retention in grade was a positive practice in the best interests of student learning and self-concept. That is, students who were allowed to move ahead to the next grade, although they were not doing satisfactory work in their present grade, learned more the next year when promoted than if they had been retained. In addition, students who have been retained once have a high probability of dropping out of school altogether at a later date. Student retention is among the few topics in schooling that have been researched quite thoroughly. Once again, we recommend that student retention in the grades be disestablished as an elementary school policy.

Positive Efforts toward Resolving Problems Related to Promotion and Retention

Retention of a student and just providing "more of the same" is a likely recipe for failure. In such cases, attention should be given to determining the causes of the learning problems. For example, if the cause of failure is due to lack of adequate work-study skills, this cause must be adequately attended. New treatments must be implemented and then assessed for successful results. Of course, promoting the student to the next grade without taking measures to improve the student's study skills, in this case, would also result in unsatisfactory learning results.

The effort to find the student's success level by increasingly providing more complex experiences that the student can perform successfully is warranted. Although merely eliminating automatic promotion is one option being practiced in education, it will not resolve the learning problems being encountered. Although social promotion is one answer to retention, placing the student in the next grade leaves the student with the same problem that was inhibiting learning previously. Determining, assessing, and evaluating the learner's problems are keys to improvement. Identifying and then correcting learning problems must be viewed as one of the teacher's primary responsibilities.

Previously, the controversy of open and ungraded classroom organizations was discussed in chapter 1. Non-graded organization, for example, can serve to place emphasis on individualization and determining the student's learning activities at his or her success level. One can find many citations in the literature regarding the contention that education should center on the needs and interests of the student. Student failure does not appear to meet this provision. "Alternate programs which allow for differing progress and needs of pupils can serve to encourage potential dropouts to remain in some formal school setting" (Norton, 1984, 20–21).

The Educational Controversy of Students' Use of Social Media

If one were to ask a student in the school about social media, the response without much question would be "great." Ask the school principal or a teacher, and both would most likely would refer to it as the school's major problem. The use of social media increasingly is the cause for student suspension hearings. Before considering selected pluses and minuses of social media in education, an actual case of its negative outcomes is presented in the following scenario.

Several students of a large high school were staying all night at the home of one of the students. The group had spent several hours between 11:30 p.m. and 4:30 a.m. enjoying contacting others with messages of various kinds. At one point in the early morning hours, they sent a message to schoolmates as follows: "Don't go to school on Thursday, there will be a shooting at 9:45 a.m." While most students were in school the next morning, a later follow-up media message read, "You have 13 minutes to live. Leave the school for home with your parents." Dozens of images were sent. Students panicked and ran in droves from the school building. Chaos was rampant.

Although tracing social media messages is difficult, forensic techniques are now available to help identify media callers. In this case, the false message of a planned school killing was traced to the home of one of the high school students. At the follow-up student suspension hearing, the accused student said, "I went to bed early. I did not know about the media messages and did not participate in them." At the time of this writing, the hearing officer was just completing the report of the hearing for the school board's review and decision of this major social media matter. Hearing officers do not make decisions regarding the guilt or innocence of the "defendant." The hearing officer conducts the hearing procedures and writes the report as to what was said by both parties at the hearing. In turn, the local school board reviews the officer's report and then makes a decision as to what action will be taken.

The Pros of Social Media Use in Schools

- Social media provide an easy way to keep in touch with family and friends. News about various matters is readily available. Friendships can be retained with those near and far.
- Social media can be much more than just entertainment. It is educational in so many ways.
- Social media sites are expanding to include information for health and medical purposes (drug addiction, weight loss, disease prevention, and many others).
- Social media allow a person to get breaking news much faster. It is great for getting immediate reports on news and sports.
- It has been reported that social media can serve to solve crimes more quickly by use of forensic techniques that track the source of users.
- Some services are in place to monitor and detect fraud.
- Education leaders stress the importance of collaboration. What source is better than social media to make new friends and improve relationships?
- Social media can give a person a support group that is not readily found offline.

- Health information available on social media can be readily obtained whereby appointments with doctors are not always available to all persons.
- Social media are essential for professional growth, curriculum planning, and student engagement. It holds endless possibilities.
- Social media connect students, teachers, administrators, and parents. What other activity can achieve such important communication?

The Cons of Social Media Use in Schools

- So much social network is almost too much to receive and share. Too much time is wasted.
- Face-to-face communication is missing. Personal relationships are inhibited.
- Social media leave one open to problems of predators, pedophiles, and the spreading of threats and dangerous information. Some services are not in place to monitor and detect fraud.
- Much false information is disseminated.
- Using social media reduces the quality of student work. Those who use it, according to reports, are at GPAs of 3.06. Others are at GPAs of 3.82.
- Use of social media can result in increased depression and other mental health difficulties according to some medical reports.
- Cyber-bullying is rampant on social media. This has to be stopped!
- Social media are dominating a student's life attention. Certainly, there are far more important life responsibilities, satisfaction, and growth opportunities available to students that should be pursued.

The Education Debate Regarding Local Control of Education

In brief, the debate concerning the federal mandating of the core curriculum is underscored by the historical concept of *local control*. Education historically has been viewed as a federal concern, a state responsibility, and a local function. The term *local function* commonly refers to the concept that schools are governed and administered by elected and sometimes appointed representatives on school boards located within the school district. School boards are governance bodies that can approve educational policy, enact taxes to support schools, and in fact serve as the legislative body of the school district. The superintendent of the school district serves as the executive officer of the district and acts to develop regulations that serve to implement approved school policies.

The primary arguments center on the belief that local school boards have "given up" or lost their leadership role in establishing viable school policies that serve to guide the school programs. For example, many school boards are purchasing their school district policies from state school board associations rather than establishing viable school district guidelines themselves. Failure to develop local policies and the increase in mandates from the state legislature have served to lessen the authority of school boards. It is not unusual to find the same school policies for almost all of the school districts in any one state.

Policies are principles/aims adopted by the school board to underscore purposes the school district wants to achieve. Policies are general in nature and call for a course of action to be taken by the school administration in meeting the desired purpose of the education program. A policy is a broad statement that allows for freedom of interpretation and execution. It is mainly the concern of the school board and is related to the question of what to do (Norton, 2017). One common requirement for being a school board member is that he or she resides in the school district being served. Thus, local control infers that the school board is in the best position to meet the school community's primary educational needs and interests.

When external state or federal agencies mandate curricular and instructional school requirements, then local control is diminished. We contend that the primary responsibility of the local school board is to develop effective school policy. The administrative staff of the school district becomes responsible for developing viable administrative regulations that serve to implement the policies set forth. It is understood that the school board receives its authority from the state legislature. In turn, the school board delegates the responsibility for regulation development to the school superintendent and professional staff. This procedure demonstrates local control. When this procedure is violated, loss of local control becomes problematic.

Nevertheless, there is considerable debate as to the extent that school boards are doing their job. This contention is focused primarily on the fact that student academic performance has been viewed as being unsatisfactory and that other state and federal agencies must intervene if this unfortunate condition is to be reversed. The pro and con arguments related to local control of education are given next.

The Pro Views for Retaining/Increasing Local Control

- Local control is predicated on the belief that school boards consist of individuals who reside within the school community and therefore are in the best position to know the educational needs and interests of students in residency.
- Experience and related evidence make it clear that local school boards and administrative staff personnel are in a much better position to attend to the local executive, judicial, and legislative matters involved in governing

a local school district than external state or federal agencies. Yet, such attention is often overlooked and left to the external state and federal agencies to attend.
- State departments are ill-equipped to be effective at the local school level for the many school districts within any one state. State department education boards are really not geared to a local school context. Emphasis of the state tends to be on standards and tests rather than on the local needs and interest of the local community.
- Reports on school effectiveness have shown that school improvement is best when the local school district is given the responsibility and support to assume the full leadership for educational outcomes.
- Educational researchers have recommended more emphasis on local school control, not less. External controls through state mandates are far more likely to fall of their own weight (Shannon, 1985).
- The recent increasing intervention of state and federal agencies into local school education has tended to lessen, not increase, the quality of local school education.
- The failure of the state and federal agencies to provide sufficient funding for local school support has lessened local school's ability to improve. With adequate funding, local school control provides the best chance for becoming the best in the world.
- If the school board is not accessible to the local citizenry, it is the voters' rights to replace them for members who focus on the purposes of student academic success.

The Con Views against Retaining/Increasing Local Control

- Local school boards have failed to provide the leadership for improving student academic performance. Therefore, external state and federal intervention has become necessary.
- Local school boards have yielded their policy-making responsibilities to external associations. Thus, they have lost their local control authority.
- The evidence concerning the lowering academic status of America's students in relation to students in other countries has resulted in a loss of confidence in local school control. State and federal intervention is necessary.
- Local school boards have not dealt satisfactorily with the many national problems such as special student needs, civil rights, student rights, bilingual education, and other national issues. State and federal intervention is necessary.

- Local school community resistance to fund education has increased the involvement of state financial support with corresponding state control.
- Current minimal requirements for school board membership inhibit school board qualifications for dealing with the growing complex issues facing education. Thus, local boards have become followers as opposed to leaders in policy development and determining those goals and objectives needed for quality programs.
- Students today are far more mobile than only a few years ago. The concept of preparing them according to the culture of the local community is flawed. Not only will the majority of students leave their school community upon graduation, but they will also live in many different states during their lifetime.

It appears to be obvious that local control of education will not continue as it has been historically. From the historical concept that education is a federal concern, state responsibility, and local function, the concept has reached the point of being a concern, responsibility, and function of all three levels of government.

We are not in favor of a national curriculum. However, a way must be found for the federal government to express its concerns without mandating federal controls. State legislatures should continue to stress the major objectives to be attained educationally, and local school boards assume the leadership in determining the curricular programs under the administration of effective school administrators and teachers. Our recommendations clearly resemble those of Michael Kirst (1988) set forth more than three decades ago.

SELF-CONTAINED VS. OPEN CLASSROOM

In the late 1950s and early 1960s the concepts of the open classroom and the ungraded school were being recommended. The rationale for such arrangements was due in part to the wide range of reading abilities within the elementary school grades. For example, it was common to find the reading levels of pupils in grade three to range from a grade one to a grade six level. There were other expressed advantages of having an open classroom arrangement including the idea that high-quality teachers could be made available to pupils in more than one grade. In the following section, the controversy of the open classroom vs. the traditional or closed classroom is considered.

Although the open classroom concept historically has been adopted and then discarded in some schools nationally, the idea presently is being promoted in some university teacher preparation programs under the guise of reimagining education. In any case, the concept of the open classroom vs. the traditional classroom arrangement is under debate today. An open classroom commonly is defined as an innovative approach in elementary schools whereby learning is viewed as being less structured and focused on the student's individual needs and interests. Several groups of students participate in a variety of activities by moving from one activity to another. Thus, the open classroom permits a more flexible system of education; it replaces the traditional subject-centered studies found in the traditional classroom.

The traditional classroom model has been in place for decades in the large majority of school classrooms. It has all students in one grade together for learning at the elementary school level and, at the middle and secondary school levels, all students of one subject in one room for learning a particular subject such as math, science, social studies, and English. The teacher provides the instruction, and the communication between and among the teacher and students is face-to-face.

We focus our attention on the pros and cons of the open classroom concept.

Often-Stated Pros of the Open Classroom Concept

- In the open classroom concept, you know what's going on around you. You can often pick up good ideas from other teachers.
- You can learn to adjust to the different activity arrangements. The concept itself begins to grow on you.
- You are able to have open sessions with parents. It fosters collaboration with parents and students.
- It opens the door for students' creativity and fosters self-learning.
- Students are able to move around and to explore their own interests.
- The opportunity for the student to learn at his or her own success level is made more possible in the open classroom.
- Teacher relations are promoted. We have only talked about the need for collaboration. In the open classroom, collaboration is practiced.
- A high-quality teacher is made more available to more students.
- The open classroom permits far more opportunities for individualized instruction.
- The informality of the open classroom enables students to move from one activity to another. Interest is enhanced and apathy is seldom observed.

The Often-Stated Cons of the Open Classroom Concept

- The open classroom can be very loud. You don't feel free to make a lot of noise with instructional activities.

- Teachers feel that they are being spied upon.
- The open classroom can be disruptive. Sometimes one must raise one's voice to be heard.
- Collaboration can also be an obstruction when it comes to students' individual tasks.
- There is a lack of research behind the idea. Since it was initiated in some schools several years ago and then discontinued, why do we not have some research information regarding the effectiveness of this concept?
- Noise is the number-one negative factor of the concept. Noise becomes too loud and distracting.
- Teachers tend to retain their closed-door classroom methods.
- Walls are created anyway. Bulletin boards, stacked-up crates, metal cabinets, bookcases, shelves, and other things hanging down serve as division walls to form separate classrooms.

It is clear that the open classroom has some basis for controversy. However, new programs will be initiated and some practices will not survive. The missing link in this case, as well in education in general, is education's curse; the lack of "Valid and reliable RESEARCH!"

The Controversy Surrounding Bilingual Education

Believe it or not! Congress passed a bill more than 50 years ago to provide bilingual education for helping some students improve their limited ability to use the English language. Sixty years later, the Bilingual Act re-emphasized the need to give English-deficient students the education needed to help them become English-proficient. But at that time in 1974, major controversy centered on the question as to if such instruction in a foreign language should take place or even be considered. The debate as to the viability of bilingual education centered on the contentions that: (1) bilingual education was far too costly; (2) bilingual education had been ineffective; and (3) there was a shortage of qualified bilingual teachers to "man" the program. Poor test scores were sufficient evidence enough to show that bilingual education should not be continued.

Supporters of bilingual education center their position on the principle of student rights: the opportunity to have a fair and equal chance for a quality education. As set forth in law, "Where inability to speak and understand the English language excludes national origin minority groups from effective participation in the education program offered by a school district, the district must take affirmative steps to rectify the language deficiency in order to open its instructional program to these students."

As pointed out in an article by Education World (2013), the U.S. Department of Education Office of Bilingual Education and Minority Language Affairs pointed out two basic principles: "(1) All children are capable of engaging in complex thinking tasks. (2) Developing and maintaining the [student's] native language in no way interferes with English language acquisition. On the contrary, research over the last decade in bilingual classrooms with established models of instructional excellence indicates that utilization of and facility in the primary language enhances the acquisition of a second language" (1).

Before summarizing the pros and cons of bilingual education, the three basic methods used in programs of bilingual education are summarized (Floriello, 2018):

Immersion—The mode of instruction is English. Teachers use easy-to-understand expressions that are especially intended to allow students to comprehend English while learning other disciplines as well.
Transition bilingual education—This method comprises some instruction in the student's native language and, simultaneously, uses a more focused English instruction.
Development or maintenance bilingual education—This approach develops the student's skills through providing instruction in their native language and teaching English as a second language (3).

The Cons Position on Bilingual Education

- No research is available that supports the fact that teaching students in a native language helps them to better learn English or other subjects.
- Many students have succeeded without being involved in bilingual education programs.
- English immersion programs have proven to be more effective than any bilingual education programs.
- Experience has clearly demonstrated that bilingual programs are ineffective and far too costly. Funding bilingual programs takes money away from other important courses such as music, art, and physical education.
- Parents of students of Hispanic origin, who used to strongly support bilingual education, have expressed skepticism about its effectiveness.
- Low test scores have demonstrated the fact that non-native English-speaking students leave schools with unsatisfactory reading proficiency in English as well as their native language.
- Some polls have revealed the fact that the majority of citizens rule against bilingual education programs in our schools. The majority should rule.

- Student time on bilingual education hinders the student's ability to work on other programs more related to their career interests.
- Focusing on bilingual education inhibits the student's need to learn more about the culture in which they now live. This tends to widen the cultural gap.

The Pros Position on Bilingual Education

- The large majority of professional teachers support bilingual education; teachers know best.
- Those persons who have claimed success without having bilingual education have had access to other resources in the home, neighborhood, books, and other learning resources.
- Bilingual education serves the American principle of equal opportunities for all. It serves as one of a student's overall rights. A school district must take positive steps to resolve the language deficiency of some students in order to enable them to engage in the educational opportunities available to other students. It is an equity matter.
- Criticizing the results of bilingual education programs is premature. Many nonproficient students learn conversational English in a relatively short period of time. However, learning academic English takes much longer. School tests commonly are administered too early. Given more time, English immersion will produce positive results.
- Immersion in English programs has many positive outcomes, one of which is the retention of students in school.
- Children who learn to speak another language or multiple languages will become a valuable community on the job market.
- There is some evidence that a child who receives a bilingual education is also less likely to experience a wide variety of personal disorders, including anxiety.
- Bilingual education leads to a more well-rounded child and adult.
- Research shows that because bilingual students are able to use two languages at the same time, it develops skills for functions such as inhibition, switching attention, and working memory (Bonfiglio, 2016).

There has been some research in the area of bilingual education programs with mixed results. As concluded by Faltis (2011), "Based on the mixed results of so many different studies, no model can be declared a winner conclusively. The varying results of the research studies leave the question of the effectiveness of bilingual education unresolved" (1). The difficulty, in part, is illustrated in the following statement.

> However, within Texas, some models show better results than others—as evidenced by research of Rossell, who found that the bilingual models in Texas did not perform well. Multiple researchers have questioned the effectiveness of transitional models. Although most of their research finds better results with sheltered or structured English immersion, Baker and Rossell do occasionally find a positive result from bilingual education. (Faltis, 2011, 88)

Thus, the controversy continues, and the debate goes on. In fact, over the years, the opposition to bilingual programs has increased.

Controversial Issues about Student Grading

The review of the literature concerning the topic of student grading turned up a volume of articles with the following titles: "Teachers Divided Over Controversial 'No-Zero Grading Policy,'" "New Grading System Causes Controversy at Windermere High School in Orange County," "The Continuing Controversy Over Grades," "English Grading System Causes Controversy," "How Many Marks Out of Ten? A Hard Look at Marking and Grading Systems," "Controversial Issues in Education: Grading Systems," "For Students' Sake, Say No to 'No Zero Policy' on Grading," "Should the Grading System be Abolished? The Controversial Grading Scale," and many others.

The literature on student grading is prolific. Just about everything imaginable on student grading has been discussed in the literature. What's left? What is left is the development of a model of student grading that does what a grading system should do and is favored by the large majority of teachers, parents, students, and members of the citizenry. This section opens with a brief history of grading in elementary and secondary schools in America. This discussion is followed by a presentation of several grading methods that have been introduced in schools nationally. A pro and con section sets forth the opinions generally expressed in favor or disfavor of student grading practices in schools.

A BRIEF HISTORY OF GRADING IN K–12 SCHOOLS

Willian Farish, a tutor at Cambridge University in 1792, is credited for inventing grades (Hartman, 2012). However, Lassahn (n.d.) stated that letter grades were first used in the late nineteenth century. She notes that both colleges and high schools began replacing various forms of student assessment with letter and percentage grades in the early part of the twentieth century. At this time in history, elementary and secondary schools in America began the initiation of grading systems into their programs. As populations increased nationally, so did the student population in local school districts. These events, along with the initiation of compulsory attendance laws, led to the necessity of building new schools. Written descriptions of student progress were reduced in favor of using both letter grades and percentage to indicate the status of a student's achievement.

As would be expected, the standards and specifications for determining a student's grade varied widely. The question of subjectivity also entered the picture. These facts led to the redesigning of grade scales, letter grades, pass and fail grading, and concepts of no grades. Each concept became targets for controversies that continue today. The purpose of grading always becomes a necessary consideration in discussions of grading in schools. Is grading to reveal: What a student has learned? How intelligent the student is in a subject? A rating that gives an indication of the student's success in college or in a career? Or just a score on a standardized test or final course examination?

A presentation of the pros and cons on student grading becomes difficult due to the fact that one has to know what grading model or system is being assessed. This problem is most difficult and leads to our decision to describe several grading systems in place in schools today.

Sosnowski (2018) identifies three specific types of grading systems. The Norm-Referenced Grading Systems serves to compare a student's achievement to that of his or her peers. "A norm-referenced system relies partially on student performance and partially on the performance of classmates" (1). "A Criterion-Referenced System focuses on specific information that students attain through the learning process" (2). In this system, the teacher determines the skills needed for what the students are to learn and the tasks that students must perform to learn these skills. Commonly, a number point is used to determine the letter grade to be received. For example, the highest grade of A might require 90 to 100 points, a grade of B would require 80 to 89 points, a grade of C would require 70–79 points, and so forth.

Other systems of grading used in practice are pass or fail systems or designations such as satisfactory or unsatisfactory. Each of these grading systems set forth is based on a percentage number that is required to pass the course. In some cases, descriptive terms are used to describe the student's performance such as "high achievement," "satisfactory achievement," and "unsatisfactory achievement." These grading systems require the identification of what course activities (e.g., quizzes, homework, required tests) determine the student's grade and the percentage that each activity counts in the final grade (e.g., quizzes are worth 20 percent, homework is worth 20 percent, and test scores are worth 60 percent).

Although the foregoing system of grading appears to be straightforward and objective, it, like all systems, is subject to controversy. One persistent argument is that some students, while performing well in other academic areas, simply do not perform well within the exam/test medium. What about the student's oral performance in the classroom? Who is doing the student's homework at home? How are student absences and missed quizzes/tests considered?

The following section sets forth examples of the pros and cons commonly stated in regard to student grading in general.

Common Cons Argued in Relation to School Grading Systems

- Grading systems consists of too many subjective inconsistencies. Thus, grades fail to reveal what the student is learning.
- Grading is focused on credentialing more than on an assessment of what the student has learned.
- The variations in how teachers assess student learning and what factors are included in the assessment leave grade outcomes unreliable for transferring records or diagnosing student learning difficulties.
- Grade inflation is taking place due to the emphasis being placed on college grants and college entrance. The result is a pressure to raise grades so that students can enter colleges of choice.
- Grading practices such as no-zero policies put struggling students in a poor position for future success in their careers of interest.
- There are too many nonacademic factors included in a teacher's assignment of grades. For example, student citizenship, attendance, class participation, apathy, and other factors tend to enter the teacher's mind when assigning grades.
- Commonly, each teacher has his or her own standards for grading. A school has 30 teachers, and each one has his or her own standards for grading. The variances are troublesome when it comes to assessing the learning factor.
- Setting policies such as "no child left behind" or setting a policy that no child receives a grade lower than 50 percent if some attempt to learn is evident is contrary to the purposes of grading for determining the extent that learning has taken place.

Common Pros Argued in Relation to School Grading Systems

- There are grading systems that are effective and relatively easy to implement. For example, two-box grading, whereby descriptions such as Pass and Pass with Merit, has several advantages. For example, the parents and

student know that the work has been done satisfactorily with some indication that the work accomplished was especially well done.
- A pass/fail grading system serves to reduce student stress and increases group cohesion. The student receives course credit without worrying about getting a grade of A, B, C, and so on. Thus, a pass/fail system allows students to engage in learning a way that is best for them.
- In a pass/fail system there is no worry about knowing everything, but one learns enough to get credit for the course. In mathematics, for example, great emphasis seems to be placed on knowing all about the quadratic equation. How many students have had to know and use this equation during their lifetime?
- Traditional grading systems are universally recognized. Everyone knows that a grade of A is good and an F is failing.
- Traditional grading systems are easy to interpret and understand. It is user friendly.
- Traditional grading systems allow for direct comparison from one student to another. Grade point averages are easily determined and easy to understand.
- In a traditional grading system, a student with a grade of A is performing better than a student with a C grade. Or, a student with a grade of 90 is performing better than a student with a grade of 70. Parents and students are more able to understand this form of grading.
- Grading can serve as a motivator for the student to learn. Receiving good grades leads to wanting to get even better grades.
- Grading results can give a student a feeling of accomplishment just like doing well in a sports activity or being recognized for one's performance in art or music.
- Grades are the foundation of academic society. Students study harder to get good grades.

In summarizing this section on the controversies of student grading, we turn to some recommendations set forth by Townsley and Buckmiller (2016). This article included 30 references on the topic of student grading. The purpose of the article was to provide an overview of the research literature on the topic of standards-based grading.

Townsley and Buckmiller note that traditional grading practices perhaps were appropriate for measuring how a student was doing in school years ago, but today grading experts agree teachers should upgrade their grading practices by aligning them with the realities of how and what students are learning in schools now. The calls for accountability in educational practices make it necessary for school professional personnel to shift their grading procedures whereby these practices center on measuring student progress and developing talent rather than just sorting it.

Standards-based principles, according to Townsley and Buckmiller, incorporate three distinct principles: (1) Grades should have meaning. They should provide meaningful feedback to students, document their learning progress, and help teachers make decisions about what the student needs to do to continue his or her learning progress; (2) grades should provide the student multiple opportunities to demonstrate learning based on feedback; and (3) teachers should put things like homework, extra credit, and helping other students on assignments in their proper place. Townsley and Buckmiller give due credit to Guskey and Bailey (2001), Marzano (2000), Dueck (2014), and O'Connor (2019), and others for their contributions to the research on the grading question. For example, Guskey, Jung, and Swan (2011) found that both teachers and parents were virtually unanimous in agreeing that standards-based grading reports provided better information as well as provided more understandable information for parents, students, and others concerned.

Controversies surrounding Class Size and Teacher Workload

The controversies surrounding class size and teacher workload differ from most other educational controversies in that considerable research has been completed on these two somewhat related issues. Yet, one of the most publicized studies on class size by Glass and Smith (1979) was later criticized by Hedges and Stock (1983) and by Hess (1979) as flawed.

We begin by considering the often-discussed topic of teacher workload. Teacher load includes much more than the number of students taught by the teacher in the classroom. Teacher load is of special importance since the teachers who are most qualified to carry out an effective education program in the school often are so overburdened that their efforts are forced to a level of mediocrity. So, the "debate" comes into play by asking if the load of classroom teachers should be measured and evaluated for purposes of equity.

Teacher load in general is discussed from two controversial perspectives. That is, teachers and administrators often speak of the work overload requirements of teacher personnel. Large class sizes, extracurricular assignments, ongoing needs for in-service development activities, pressures to earn additional degrees and credit hours, afterschool and evening activity requirements, and having to go to college or work other jobs for living purposes all add up to such negative results.

Criticism of the teacher's workload is voiced on several perspectives. One contention is the criticism that teachers get full compensation for teaching only 8 months of the year. That is, teachers are free during four months of the year. In addition, it is said that teachers enjoy many vacation days over the school year, including Christmas, New Years, Thanksgiving, spring vacation, and several other holidays that are celebrated in America.

The matter of class size is quite different from teacher load. Class size does not address the topic of teacher load in its full perspective. As early as 1928, Harl Douglass developed a formula to measure the teacher load of secondary school personnel. The formula has been refined, validated, and tested in hundreds of research studies over the years. Teacher load not only includes the number of students that a teacher has in the classroom but also centers on the nature of the subject taught, the number of subject preparations in the teaching assignment, the number of classes taught each week, the length of each class period, and the average number of minutes the teacher spends in nonteaching duties during the semester including afterschool activities and in-service development programs.

It is common to find survey information on teacher load issues. One survey notation indicated that heavy workloads were raising havoc among new recruits. Over 75 percent of the respondents of one survey indicated that workload was the main reason they considered leaving. A survey in the *Guardian* (2018) revealed that heavy workload was forcing new teachers out of the profession. One participant noted that the new technology was to make lives easier but concluded that it actually added to the workload.

Norton and Bria (1992) developed a formula for measuring elementary school teacher load. A full discussion of this load formula is beyond the scope of this chapter. However, the formula included the load factors of assigned hours of teaching, time spent in preparation for teaching, cooperative or extracurricular duties of non-instructional nature, the number of students taught, and the load related to extra grades taught in a single classroom by one teacher. Unlike the Douglass formula, the Norton/Bria formula measures teacher load in hours of time spent per week in teaching rather than in index load units used in the Douglass load formula.

Neither the Douglass formula nor the Norton Bria formula settles the question of how "hard" a teacher is working. Rather, both formulas do give information that shows the inequities of load among teachers within the same school setting. For example, studies of teacher load using the Douglass formula have revealed that it is not unusual to have teachers carrying the heaviest teacher loads having a load index three times that of teachers with the lowest indices. In addition, studies have revealed that commonly the load index of first-year teachers is among the highest of all teachers in the school. Perhaps this fact is part of the reason that 20 to 30 percent of first-year teachers leave the profession after one year.

Whether or not teachers are overworked or are being paid fairly in view of their actual time of employment each year is one controversial debate. One survey on teacher load found that 87 percent of the teachers in the study population knew of a teacher who left the profession due to the workload. Another 87 percent reported that they had given thought to leaving for the same reason. On the average, 90.3 percent of the teachers spent 45–55 hours per week on school work in and out of school. Ninety percent indicated that their workload had a negative effect on their personal life.

It is of some interest to find just what activities are taking up time in teachers' lives. In the aforementioned study, marking was included as a time consumer by 90.3 percent of the teachers. Planning was a time consumer of 83.3 percent, assessment was a time consumer of 68.7 percent, SAT prep was a time consumer of 16.4 percent, preparation was a time consumer for 16.0 percent, understanding was 21.7 percent, setting up instructional displays was 21.4 percent, and others received 6.2 percent. That is, many persons argue that instructional time in the classroom is not the only consideration for determining the work assignment of a professional teacher.

In closing the discussion of teacher workload, we call the reader's attention to the excellent workload survey study, Workload, Stress, and Resilience of Primary Teachers: Report of a Survey of INTO Members, an interim report to Congress 2015 (Morgan, 2015). The report provides important information related to the prevalence of stress among teachers, the effects of stress, the causes of stress, how workload stress leads to burnout, and the many changes in education over the years that have changed the workload consideration of the professional teacher. In brief, the report provides data as to how teaching has changed in regard to stress, demands, challenges, enjoyment, and rewards. In addition, the factors making teaching more or less challenging are detailed. This is a must-read publication for educators.

Key Chapter Ideas and Recommendations

- The controversial issues being encountered in education are numerous. Some debates have gone on for years, and others are relatively new to scene. These controversial issues matter for several reasons, one of which is the fact that such issues inhibit program success and student learning is affected.
- Educational controversy is especially difficult to resolve. When some resolution is recommended or a court ruling is set forth, these "resolutions" tend to conjure up further controversy.
- Although controversies in education are present in local schools, they always have implications for state and federal interests as well.
- One of the paramount needs of school programs today is sound education research. Education's lack of viable research activities that focus on controversial issues inhibits the need to find best solutions that local schools can endorse.
- In some instances, the research that is conducted on certain controversies is available but overlooked by local school leaders. Thus, schools tend to keep on doing what was in practice, and the same debates continue.

- The listing of pros and cons related to the various controversies give school leaders some basis for focusing on what problems are present and how these differences might be considered and resolved.
- Variations in school standards and administrative procedures within the several states add problems toward determining solutions that are acceptable to all concerned.
- The article by Morgan (2015) regarding the effects of teacher workload is highly recommended for educational personnel. Attention to the information in that article will serve school leaders in many ways toward resolving teacher workload problems.

Discussion Questions

1. Briefly review the several controversial education issues discussed in this chapter. Which issues, if any, are ones being faced by your school or ones for which you are most familiar? Identify any issues that the school that you have in mind has resolved or attempted to resolve. If possible, describe how this issue was ultimately resolved.
2. Assume that you have been appointed to serve on a school committee to recommend a new grading system. At present, the school uses a standard system of A-excellent to F-failure. Set forth your recommendations for the new system. What are the primary purposes underlying your recommendation for the system that you favor?
3. Chapters 1 and 2 have mentioned the need for improved research in education. Differences in opinions regarding the various controversial issues commonly have not been sufficiently researched. Give thought as to who should be doing the needed research; the local school district, the state, the federal government, the institutions of higher education? Avoid giving a general answer such as "all of them."
4. Empirical evidence has revealed that various issues that have received valid and reliable research are seldom implemented in schools. For example, if a medical cure for cancer were discovered, the results would be implemented immediately in medical practices worldwide. Why is this practice not evidenced in education? Research studies on student retention, teacher load, learning styles, and others are cases in point.
5. At a meeting of the school board, a parent makes the following statement: "Superintendent Ostenberg, tonight you mentioned something about the open classroom concept that is being implemented in some of the state's school districts. Just what is your position on this concept?" You are the superintendent, what is your response to the open classroom question? At present, the school district has the standard closed-door classrooms arrangement.

Case Study: "Principal Black, Students in Your School Are Violating the Principle of Church and State"

Emory Ross, Principal November 2, 2019
College View, Lafayette
CV High School

Dear Principal Ross:

There is a practice going on in your school that violates the U.S. Constitution. I am speaking of the group of students in the lunchroom each noon that are praying before having lunch each day. My daughter tells me that this is a group of ten or so seniors who pray out loud in the lunchroom. She informs me that other students sitting nearby can hear the words of the praying. One student is the son of Reverend Amos Jenkins of the local Presbyterian Church.

I am sending a copy of this letter to Superintendent Madeline Lyon. Both she and you should be fully aware that the U.S. Supreme Court has ruled praying in schools as unconstitutional.

Hopefully, you will stop this unlawful practice in your school immediately.

Sincerely,
Mrs. James Geston

cc: Supt. Madeline Lyon

Discussion Questions

1. Before responding to this parent, review the chapter's section on prayer in schools. What information will help you in your reply?
2. After completing the suggestion in item 1, draft your professional letter to Mrs. Geston with a copy to Superintendent Lyon.

REFERENCES

Allen, R. (2006). Intelligent design versus evolution sparks debate. *Education Update*, 48 (2).

Bonfiglio, C. (2016, July 21). *Bilingual Kidspot, the benefits of a bilingual education.* https://bilingualkidspotl.com2016/07/21/bilingual-education-benefits/.

Douglass, H. R. (1928). Measuring teacher load in high schools. *The Nation's Schools*, 2 (4), 22–24.

Education.com (2012, April 22). *Prayer in schools: Benefits from both sides.* https://supports.education.com/customer/portal/emails/new.

Ed World (2013). U.S. Office of Bilingual Education and Minority Language Affairs. worldcat.org/identities/lccn-n83-209677/.

Faltis, K. (2011). Bilingual, ESL, and proficient students in Texas. *Pepperdine Policy Review*. Malibu, CA: Pepperdine University.

Fioriello, P. (2018). *Examining both sides of the bilingual debate*, 48 (2). http://drpfconsults.com/author/dr-patricia-fioriello/.

Guskey, T. R. (1994). Making the grade: What benefits students? *Education Leadership*, 52 (2), 14–20.

Guskey, T. R., Jung, G. M., & Swan, L. A. (2011). Grades that mean something. *Phi Delta Kappan*, 93 (2), 52–57.

Hadderman, M. L. (1988). State vs. local control of schools, *ERIC Digest*, 24. https://eric.ed.gov/?id=ED291164.

Hartman, T. (2012, September 25). For the Love of Learning. An excerpt from *Complete Guide to ADHD*. https://www.amazon.com/Thom-Hartmans-complete-guide-ADHD/dp/.

Hedges, L. V., & Stock, W. (1983, January 1). The effects of class size: An examination of rival hypotheses. *American Educational Research Journal*. https://doi.org/10.3102/0028312020001063.

Hess, F. (1979). Class size revisited: Glass & Smith in perspective, *ERIC Clearinghouse*, 11.

Kirst, M. W. (1988). Who should control our schools? *NEA Today*, 6, 74–79.

Lassahn, N. (n.d.). History of grading systems. *Classroom* (blog), by Leaf Group Education. https://classroom.synonym.com/history-grading-systems-5103640.html.

Morgan, M. (2015). *Workload, stress, and resilience of primary teachers: Report of a survey of INTO members.* Interim Report to Congress 2015. Mark Morgan with the assistance of the Education Committee of the INTO working group and Head Office staff.

Norton, M. S. (1983, Summer). It's time to get tough on student promotion—Or is it? *Contemporary Education*, LIV (4).

Norton, M. S. (1984). Student promotion and retention. *The Education Digest*, XLIX (5). Ann Arbor, MI: Prakken Publications, Inc.

Norton, M. S. (2017). *A guide for educational policy governance: Effective leadership for policy development.* Lanham, MD: Rowman & Littlefield Publishers.

Norton, M. S., & Bria, R. (1992). Toward an equitable measure of elementary school teacher load. *Record in Elementary Education and Supervision*, 13(1), 62–66.

Ridder, K. (2014, November 24). *Supreme Court rulings on prayer in public schools: 5 facts about historic cases*. West Palm Beach, FL: Newsmax Media, Inc., Independent American.

Shannon, T. A. (1985). A 1985 Fairy Tale. Phi Delta Kappan66 (1985), 497–500.

Sosnowski, J. (2018, September 5). Types of grading systems. *Classroom,* (blog), by Leaf Group Education. https://classroom.synonym.com/types-grading-systems-5372186.html.

Townslery, M., & Buckmiller, T. (2016, January 14). "What does the research say about standards-based grading? A research primer." http://works.bepress.com/matt-townsley/5/.

Weinstein, A. (2012, April 3). 5 most controversial issues in U.S. education. *Listosaur*. https://listosaur.com/miscellaneous/5-most-controversial-issues-in-us-education/.

Wikipedia, (2018, July 21). *Creation and evolution in public education.* https://en.wikipedia.org/wiki/Creation_and_evolution_in_public_education.

Chapter 3

Educational Controversies at the State Level

Primary Chapter Goal: To identify selected educational controversies of primary concern of the several states and to present the pros and cons of the debates along with available information related to each selection.

The selection of educational controversies that are being encountered at the state level carries with them the fact that almost every state controversy has related concerns at the local school and federal government levels as well. Prayer in schools, inclusive schools, school funding, student health, school busing for purposes of integration, student rights, and special education are local school examples that most assuredly influence practices at the state level as well. In addition, state education policies are subject to the rulings of federal laws, the higher courts, and the interpretations of the U.S. Constitution. Federal educational "policies" also have major effects on state educational legislation. For state and local educational bodies to take advantage of federal legislative programs on education, for example, they must comply with all federal requirements in order to receive the federal monetary support.

Before discussing several controversial issues facing the states, a brief history of the states' educational offices is necessary. Since the U.S. Constitution does not mention education, education has been considered as one of the matters left to the states and the people under the Tenth Amendment: The powers not delegated to the U.S. Constitution, or prohibited, are reserved to the states or to the people. In fact, the states, constitutionally, have 100 percent of the educational policy authority. Local school boards have those powers that are delegated to them by the state legislature. Of course, the local school board must comply with state or federal ruling unless the U.S. Supreme Court rules otherwise.

A BRIEF HISTORY OF THE EDUCATION DEPARTMENTS WITHIN THE STATES

Perhaps the most comprehensive review of the institution role of state education departments was authored by Thomas B. Timar (1997) of the University of California at Riverside. This scholarly historical document is one that should be on the desk of every state legislator, state of education department employee, and other state agency members that have a concern for the effective school programs in school districts in America.

A full report of Timar's article is beyond the scope of this chapter. However, important conclusions regarding the leadership of state education offices are presented here. Timar points out that a major cause of the weakness of state education departments is the well-preserved tradition of local control. This is because state governments have never seen fit to adequately invest in the agencies that are primarily responsible for supporting educational improvements.

Historically, state education agencies have had to play different roles at times. A role of service at one time in history centered on the state's direct support of educational operations at the local level. Later in history, control became the primary role of state educational agencies. Concerns for certain national needs, including vocational education, special student needs programs, academic improvements for K–12 learners, integration, and other national concerns, found their way into the role of state education agencies. In each and every historical role of state legislatures, politics have weighed heavily on the outcomes of intended purposes.

Timar notes that organizational tinkering, rather than defined systematic reform, has been in evidence in state department's organization. Roles have changed as external circumstances have changed. The constraints on state agencies have been political rather than organizational. Thus, the contention on one hand has been that what state agencies have been doing is easily erased. So, one of the ongoing controversies is whether or not state educational agencies are necessary: that they are unnecessary and do nothing but drain the public purse. One early historical "con" contention accused the well-known educator Horace Mann of creating godless schools. That is, he and other persons were trying to banish the Bible from schools.

The conclusion of Timar's historical report suggests that sustained, long-term institutional reform within state educational agencies is unlikely without a strong state infrastructure on which to build. The continuous changes in political influences will continue to inhibit such a positive outcome. Recent state elections have shown an increase in the number of educators on the ballots for election for state legislative offices. Reportedly, in Oklahoma, the number of educators in the legislatures nearly tripled, from 9 to 25 (Schnell, 2018).

The Pro Contentions for the Effective Continuation of State Education Departments

- State departments serve not only to interpret and facilitate the development of educational legislation but also to observe its effects and to implement mandates. This purpose serves a need of paramount importance.
- There is a need for a central office that has the education knowledge and skills to serve in a capacity to resolve controversies that inevitably occur between school districts and other regional and state agencies.
- State departments of education can serve a vital role in the implementation of services set forth by the state legislature.
- There is a leadership role needed to promote, assess, and evaluate improvement in education by helping to unite all forces within the state toward the accomplishment of purposes and objectives; the state department serves in a leadership position to achieve this end.
- The concept that education is a state function was established by the U.S. Constitution. Since that time, this concept has expanded within the power of the states by way of state constitutions and positive state legislative and judicial practices.
- Historically, the concept of education as a state responsibility has become deeply rooted in the early colonial laws and continued in the territorial laws and ordinances that later were continued in the states.
- Some of education's early leaders such as Horace Mann and Henry Barnard worked to improve the weakness and strengths of education. Such leadership led to the establishment of state education departments that have served in similar ways to improve education in America.

The Con Contentions for the Disbanding of State Departments of Education

- Various assumptions of responsibility regarding the failure of local schools have placed state education departments into negative relationships with local school districts. Rather than providing support services, state education agencies have polluted the relationships with local school districts.
- The courts and federal government agencies have drawn state education offices into procedural, political, and technological roles that have added to the controversies facing them.
- State education departments can be challenged regarding their competency to manage the new demands facing education. The record shows clearly that state educational personnel are ill-equipped to handle the issues/problems facing schools today.

- The concept of state service and support has been dissolved, and personnel are no longer accountable to the local citizenry and their local school districts.
- State departments of education have become primarily a dispenser of federal funds and as such are of little or no value to local school districts educationally. The role of monetary funding can be easily administered by other existing state agencies at a much lower cost.
- Large differences of opinion exist as to just how much authority should be extended by state departments of education. Recent oversight regarding student academic testing requirements is a case in point. The testing mandates are flawed. Local school districts are in a much better position to determine the best education programs for students in the local school community.
- The main groups that are destroying positive relationships with local school personnel, parents, school boards, and teachers are state boards of education and state departments of education. Shutting down local schools and removing licensing of principals whose schools have "failed" testing requirements have served as oppressing factors for needed cooperative educational solutions for issues facing the local schools.
- Anyone who praises state departments of education for their leadership mandates on academic testing should read Chris Carter's article, "The Case against Standardized Tests" (n.d.). Carter's research demonstrates the lack of validity of standardized testing results.
- There is no research to support the effectiveness of state education departments and their functions or their existence.
- State school board members commonly are appointed by the governor according to the political party in office. Politics rather than educational expertise determine what educational practices will be in place.
- No state board member is on record for asking important questions regarding such matters as Common Core; they simply follow the party line's position.
- State education boards tend to look to the federal government for direction rather than consulting with parents, administrators, and teachers in their own school district.

Research Related to the Work of State Education Departments/Agencies

The assessment and evaluation of the pro and con "arguments" on the efficacy of the work of state departments of education perhaps are best determined by one's personal assessment of the pro and con "arguments" set forth in the foregoing chapter information. Attempting to research the viability of state departments of education tends to be somewhat an exercise in futility. Of course, the attainment of the goals and objectives of a state department could be assessed and evaluated, but the goals and objectives of the department would certainly be contested by local school districts and other groups and individuals.

Our Recommendation

We are not in favor of a national curriculum. However, a way must be found for the federal government to express its major educational concerns in broad statements that allow for freedom of the states to interpret and execute them. Federal broad-purpose statements should give direction to the states for ameliorating an educational issue/problem of major importance to the nation. In turn, legislatures and state departments of education should continue to stress the major educational purposes to be attained. The state policies should also be general in nature leaving room for discretional freedom of local school boards to develop and execute.

Local school boards assume the leadership in determining the primary curricular program purposes for the state's education program. These policies serve to answer the question of "what to do." The local school administration and professional staff then develop administrative regulations for implementing the school board's policies. Administrative regulations are precise; they call for a specific interpretation and execution. Regulations are related to the question of "how to do."

VOCATIONAL EDUCATION

Vocational education has historically been an important but a controversial topic in the United States. Not only is the debate about what is to be offered in a vocational program but how such programs are to be delivered, what education level of students are to be involved, who is to deliver them, and how are these programs to be funded are debates of primary importance.

We have selected an example that serves to demonstrate the kinds of controversies that are commonly encountered in vocational education programs. In 2012, for example, an article by Dana Goldstein pointed out the controversies related to vocational education that took place during the Obama administration. In the article, "The Future of Vocational Education," Arne Duncan, the then secretary of education, set forth the administration's plan: not the state's plan, but the federal vocational education plan.

The plan proposed to invest $1 billion to increase partnerships between high schools, colleges, and employers, with the goal of directing students toward high-needed industries such as engineering and healthcare. The federal plan, of course, directly placed the federal government into the curricular programs that would take place in the states and local schools of the nation. As would be expected, the announcement of the federal plan was received as having too much of a focus on post-high-school occupational training and not enough on introducing younger adolescents to the world of work outside the classroom (Goldstein, 2012).

Additional follow-up of the plan and its controversies are beyond the scope of this chapter.

Nevertheless, the foregoing history does offer information about the problems of vocational education and its intervention into both state and local programs since its major adoption into education programs in the early twentieth century. In 1917, the Smith-Hughes Act, a federal legislative act, became the first law to authorize federal funding for vocational education in schools of the United States. The Perkins Act of 1990 attempted to reconcile the many controversial problems relating to such matters as meeting the needs of students, reducing the overcrowded traditional classrooms in secondary schools, and meeting the demands for skilled workers in the growing industries of a growing America. In every instance during the long history of vocational education, the states have been deeply involved in its controversial matters of program, student involvement, funding, and other related provisions.

THE CONTROVERSIES OF SPECIAL EDUCATION IN THE U.S.

Differences between federal and state laws are a central problem. However, the differences tend to be how the federal laws are carried out rather than debates about the laws themselves. That is, the federal laws commonly leave room for the 50 states to interpret the rules and, in turn, pass their own laws on how to apply them. This procedure is an example of the governance process that was set forth earlier in this chapter. Rosen (2014–2018) set forth several examples of the differences that are relevant to the purposes of this chapter. Two such examples are presented in the following paragraph.

As to the question of who is eligible for special education, the federal law (Individuals with Disabilities Education Act [IDEA]) specifies that students who have one of 13 types of disabilities may qualify for special education; the disability must "adversely affect" their educational performance. States can never provide less service than what is set forth in federal law, but many states have qualification guidelines for each disability listed. It is common for states to differ widely on categories as "specific learning disabilities." As a result, the term *specific learning disabilities* in one state may differ from the term used in other states nationally (Rosen, 2014–2018).

Another prime example of federal and state law differences is related to the least restricted requirement clause set forth in the federal Free and Appropriate Education (FAPE) ruling included in the Individuals with Disabilities Education Act of 1975. IDEA states that every student with a disability is entitled to a free and appropriate education; the disability must have an adverse effect on the student's ability to learn.

On the other hand, the states have used their own discretion as to just what instructional services they will provide. Of course, many different instructional models and methods might be viewed as being appropriate. However, the courts have ruled on the matter of placement of students with disabilities and, if the current placement of the disabled learner has resulted in some progress, parents have not been able to reach for other higher program placements for that child.

Once again, we underscore the fact that issues/controversies at one level, such as the state department of education, reverberate within the other levels of federal and local governments. This is the reason that a focus on special education at the state level necessitates a consideration of its implications for federal government program activities as well as program provisions at the local school level. The pro and con positions on the need/effectiveness of state departments of education concerning special education programs are stated in the following section.

Keep in mind that the pro and con positions for state responsibilities of special education are statements of opinion commonly spoken in debates on the subject. Such statements reflect the views and experiences of different groups and individuals as opposed to underscoring the results of valid and reliable research studies. The entries reveal the various controversies that appear in the literature and are present in the conversations of various local, state, and federal groups and individuals when the subject of special education is brought to the floor.

The Pro Statements for Special Education Related to State Educational Agencies

- A wide variety of special education needs are now finding their way into the program requirements of state departments of education. Progress in special education provisions during the past five decades has been made possible in large part by the leadership of state departments of education.

- State legislatures and departments, in cooperation with local school districts, have taken the leadership in assessing and evaluating the ongoing improvements in special education programming.
- The oversight of the state educational agencies has worked to make certain the right support needed for the students' disabilities is provided.
- The state educational requirements for special education serve in helping to ensure that many specialists are available to do the best for each child's needs. Counselors and other resource personnel have been made available for counseling parents and family members as well.
- Give thought to the great progress that has been made in the area of special education for special needs children within the states. Leadership by state department legislation and departments of education must be credited for these advancements.
- Local school districts are not able to deliver the needed special education services for children and youth without the support of state services.

The Con Statements Concerning the Need for
State Involvement in Special Education

- An assessment of the limited special education programs in many school districts nationally is evidence enough for noting the unsatisfactory support of state legislatures and departments. For example, too many local programs are underfunded particularly by the state government. One report estimated that 40,000 special education teachers are not fully certified to teach special education. Transition services are unsatisfactory or even missing for helping disabled students move from education to adult living. Shortages of special education teachers leave an unfair learning program for disabled students. State accountability is missing.
- State department assessment programs for disabled students are lacking and certainly not comparable to the assessment and evaluation programs being implemented for other students.
- Oversight responsibilities of state departments of education are lacking in regard to special education within the states. Many disabled students do not have access to the same curricular or extracurricular activities as other students. According to the Government Accountability Office, practices such as the restraint and seclusion of disabled students are a major source of trauma.
- State-level expenditures for special education programs are extremely costly. The funding of special education among the 50 states varies to a great extent. As a result, a special education student in one state might be better or worse off by moving to another state. Funds from the general education budget of schools commonly are used to support special education. Thus, needed funding for general education is further endangered. Available

funding for special education would be better spent if given directly to the local school districts in the state.

As is the case for the major differences for the general financial support of K–12 education among the 50 states, the financial support for special education differs greatly as well. The problem of determining equity for educational funding within the many schools in any one state has been evasive historically. Finding such equity in the financial support of special education within the states has been a controversial issue historically as well.

THE CONTROVERSIAL ISSUE OF TEACHER TENURE

Teacher tenure has been a controversial issue historically. The term *tenure* is derived from Latin meaning "to hold." That is, in K–12 educational practices, teacher tenure protects a teacher from being dismissed for unsubstantiated reasons. It serves as a policy that restricts the ability to fire teachers without a "just cause" rationale. The pros and cons on the topic of tenure are virtually unending. After an examination of the pluses and minuses regarding teacher tenure, both sides of the controversy seemingly can be accepted for different reasons.

Since the listing of pros and cons for teacher tenure is so extensive, we have chosen to refer to the listing of five major pros and five major cons on the subject set forth by Mathis (2009–2018) in her article "Teacher Tenure Debate: Pros and Cons." Mathis's brief listing sets forth both sides of the debate in a clear and fair fashion. Her pro contention entry, that teacher tenure prevents teachers from being fired for inappropriate reasons, is a case in point. Her major con entry, that almost all teachers are tenured whether deserved or not, is well expressed also.

The Pro Contentions for the Support of Teacher Tenure

- Teacher tenure prevents teachers from being fired for inappropriate reasons.
- Teacher tenure provides them with protection to take risks with new materials or learning methods, questioning decisions by the administration, or speaking out about problems without fear of reprisal.
- Teacher tenure protects them from false accusations. Teachers are often blamed for unfounded wrongdoings.
- Teacher tenure allows time for teachers to continually improve. One tends to become motivated for continuous improvement when given the perception that one is doing a good job.
- Teacher tenure provides an environment where teachers are encouraged to improve.

The Con Contentions for the Elimination of Teacher Tenure

- Almost all teachers are placed in tenure whether they really deserve it or not.
- Dismissing a teacher is extremely expensive. Reportedly, dismissal costs are upward toward $250,000 to go through the legal process of firing a teacher. Therefore, it should be discontinued with different contract provisions put into place.
- Tenure can lead to a matter of secrecy in the way of payoffs for teachers to resign rather than being fired. Thus, the teacher is free to apply and be hired in another teaching position elsewhere. Students continue to suffer.
- Tenure leads to complacency. After only three years, there is no reason to "work so hard." The teacher feels secure even though he or she knows that he or she is not giving his or her all to the job.
- Tenure simply protects bad teachers. Ultimately, the poor teacher becomes lazy; students suffer. Tenure should be replaced with one-year contracts that are easily eliminated after the first year if bad teaching is evident.

Other reasons for eliminating teacher tenure include statements of costs for the retraining of poor teachers, the damages that poor teachers can do toward disengaging students in the learning process, or, as some contend, tenure serves to reduce the quality of teaching of other teachers in the organization who tend to work at the lowest level of production of the organization. Others turn to the problem of tenure in relation to the political power of the National Education Association and Federal Teachers Association in their efforts to protect the teacher regardless of their teaching qualification.

We support the complete change in the way teachers are compensated at the time of their entry into teaching as discussed earlier in chapters 1 and 2. Changing the compensation method by paying teachers much higher rates when entering the profession not only encourages high-quality individuals to consider education as a career but also serves to retain them in the profession. Who benefits? Teachers, students, and almost everyone else. But what about costs? It is difficult to name any enterprise more important to America's future than education.

THE CONTROVERSIAL ISSUE OF STATE AND MAYORAL TAKEOVERS OF LOW-PERFORMING SCHOOLS

The events of state and mayoral school takeovers of low-performing local K–12 schools have increased dramatically during the past few decades. According to reports by Kaitlin Pennington (2014), state school takeovers have gone from attempting to create "simple' turnaround strategies to the creation of new school districts that are managed by the state. As stated by Pennington, "The new state turnover strategy varies in terms of the level of state control and local influence, and its success has been mixed or cannot yet be fully measured" (2014, 2). The success has been mixed and, as would be expected, has resulted in controversial debates.

If creating new school districts is not enough to disturb the citizenry, such outcomes as school calendar changes, schools with freedom to operate without the restrictions placed on most other school districts, experimentation with various personnel practices, curricular programs, and major attention to professional development have been present in state school takeovers. Reportedly, program success is still to be seen, but ongoing controversy is quite apparent. Some persons contend that all that is needed is more staff development. One information source reported that teacher professional development was being outsourced to external service providers.

One notable outcome of state school takeovers is the increase of approved charter schools throughout America. In most cases, charter schools operate outside the local school district's school board and have much more freedom to operate according to standards that tend to be unclear and seldom assessed. Charter schools in the United States most likely lead the list of controversial issues in education today. The support of charter schools commonly is provided by funds from state taxes. In one state, one charter school executive paid himself over $8 million in 2018. Another charter owner was indicted for improper use of state funding.

Oversight of charter schools tends to be missing. Reliable information regarding the operation, funding, expenditures, academic outcomes, and personnel in charter schools is one of education's great needs. Operating school districts directly by hiring a school leader and teacher teams and granting them charter school autonomy is the answer to quality school success, or is it? In the following section of the chapter, the pros in support of school takeovers by the state are summarized.

In the consideration of state school takeovers, we make note of the entry of city mayoral school takeovers as well. Gross (2011) noted that Chicago, Boston, New York City, and Washington, D.C., tried mayoral school takeovers before returning to a system led by an elected school board some six years later. In the following pro and con statements regarding local school takeovers, both state and mayoral takeovers are included in the support or non-support points of view. We are quite aware of differences between state and mayoral school takeovers, but controversies and debates in both activities have somewhat similar approaches and end results.

The Pros in Support of State/Mayoral Takeovers of Local Schools in the United States

- State takeovers of local schools especially have served to increase the number of charter schools substantially. Charter schools present an opportunity for new educational interventions that engage students in learning and promote effective academic learning.
- State school takeovers serve to ensure the development of positive standards for educational goals and objectives.
- State school takeovers can be kept free of local politics and influences that have tended to inhibit local school effectiveness.
- State and mayoral takeovers of local schools begin with an immediate effort to improve current unsatisfactory local school academic results.
- State controls of education at the local levels are needed for establishing positive educational standards and proper utilization of financial expenditures.
- When local school education is failing, something must be done. State legislatures are legally responsible for education within the state and are the logical bodies to takeover failing schools.
- Local school systems under mayoral control have improved local schools in terms of administrative and financial management.
- Mayoral leadership is able to provide a lot of resources both inside and outside of the local school system to address the local negative conditions/challenges that exist.
- State funds are provided for expansion and improvements of local school education.
- Takeovers have one primary purpose: to eliminate current negative educational outcomes and replace them with positive education program results for students.
- Early takeovers of local schools by external agencies represent positive steps to improve the present negative conditions at local schools that are failing.

The Cons of Non-Support of State/Mayoral Takeovers of Local Schools in the United States

- State and mayoral takeovers of local schools represent a reduction of local school control that historically has been considered to be the democratic way to include the local citizenry to vote on educational matters closely related to its needs and interests.
- State and mayoral school takeovers result in taking funds from traditional K–12 schools that are needed to achieve the improvements that are needed to remove them from a failing position.

- State and mayoral school takeovers are more of a political play to control education than to protect public education.
- Such takeovers close the door on local school boards that consist of local citizens who have students' best interests in mind. School boards have much more ownership with local education needs and interests.
- Mayoral governance of education is not the answer. Neither political parties nor its members are qualified to administer education programs at the local level.
- State and mayoral takeovers of local education circumvent the will of the people.
- Local decision about education should rest with the local citizenry.
- The idea of appointing a CEO along with an appointed school committee carries with it negative political outcomes and continuing controversial debates.
- State or mayoral control is not a panacea. What are the qualities of political appointees for administering a learning school culture in public schools?
- Such takeover systems result in resistance and mistrust with less opportunity to get work done. Cooperative relationships are extremely difficult to come by.
- Controlled state or mayoral school programs are stripped of their accreditation that leaves students without creditable credentials for higher education entrance.
- When the state or mayoral agencies take over local education, the best administrative and teaching leaves the system immediately. Students are left without qualified teachers, and other qualified personnel are reluctant to join such an undemocratic controlled organization.

We have no magic wand to resolve the controversies that exist with the issue of state and mayoral takeovers of local schools. In previous chapter discussions, we have termed one or more controversial education issues as being near or at the top of the list. Once again, we point to the controversies related to local school takeovers as at or near the most serious problems facing education today. In any case, we disfavor takeover solutions and believe that there must be much better ways toward resolving the problems of takeovers. We do know about those factors/characteristics that are evident in almost every highly effective school.

Although our recommendations for implementing effective school programs are somewhat general, the recommendations do set forth the leading success factors that must be attained if effective schools are to be attained.

1. *The highest quality of administrative, teachers, and support personnel must be present in all local school programs.* Such a goal requires the

importance of education in America for the sustaining of a democratic republic in our nation. Almost every effective K–12 program includes courses on the many areas of vocational education, business organizational practices, industrial programs, agriculture practices, government offices, social science endeavors, life sciences, the fine arts, and their life professions and careers.

Why not have courses on the profession of education? Such a program would be designed to attain three primary purposes: (1) To gain the early interest of young people in education through programs that underscore the important opportunities that it provides and encourage talented children and youth to participate in educational activities not unlike responses to early interest in nursing, law, or business enterprise; (2) to upgrade the preparation program for educational leadership toward the goal of promoting visionary leadership attitudes accompanied by extensive knowledge and experience that focus on leadership for positive change and continuous improvement; and (3) to emphasize the paramount importance of educational support by all local, state, and federal agencies for establishing a financial structure for education that ensures the attraction of high-quality personnel into the career field of professional education (Norton, 2015, 104).

2. *Effective school programs commonly have positive ties with parents and the overall school community.* Effective schools not only welcome parental involvement in their school activities but also require it as fits the case. The work life of parents tends to differ, and involvement requirements must be established with this fact in mind. The involvement of parents encompasses a variety of activities, some of which include assistance in the students' classrooms. The special talents of parents are utilized in various ways and are implemented in accord with school board and state regulations.

Local school site-based councils are required in some states. Site-based councils commonly include parent representatives, teacher representatives, student representatives, staff representatives, and the school assistant principal and principal. Site-based councils are authorized by state legislatures and the local school board and do have delegated governance authority. A positive outcome of this arrangement rests on the fact that parent members not only have the opportunity to become knowledgeable about the school's successes but also are aware of the problems that the school is encountering. In turn, these parents become effective communicators with other parents within the community.

3. *Effective school programs have comprehensive curricular and extracurricular programs that serve as the foundation for establishing a learning culture in the school.* The elected members of the school board focus on the board's primary responsibility of approving the education policies that specify what it is that the program is to achieve.

The administrative regulations for school operations become the primary responsibility of a highly competent school superintendent and professional staff. Administrative regulations serve to answer the question of how board policies are to be implemented in practice. Both documents, policies and regulations, serve to establish a comprehensive curriculum that is based on the needs and interests of students.

Effective school programs operate most effectively under policies and regulations that are drafted internally. That is, the local school board studies the school district's educational purposes and drafts policies that set forth these aims and objectives. In many states, the policies of the school district are drafted by the state's school boards association. This procedure results in the fact that almost every school district in the state has the same school policies. Local involvement in policy development is curtailed.

Effective school policies are recommended by various groups and individuals in the school district, including the school superintendent and professional staff, parent groups, community groups and individuals, and, of course, the state offices and the courts. When members of the school staff are not involved in the school policy development process, they have little or no interest in its application. Policy manuals rest on the shelves of teachers' classrooms mainly gathering dust.

4. *Effective schools commonly exist within communities that view education as an investment.* Since effective schools also engage parents and other school community members in various school programs and activities, they come to realize that schools need adequate support financially.

Bond issues and budget overrides most often are established for the purpose of constructing new schools, constructing school building additions or extensions, and completing facility repairs. Bond issue committees commonly are established to facilitate communication as to the school district's needs. It is not unusual to have community members serve on the committee with one of them serving as committee chair. The school superintendent and other school representative are available to answer questions, to provide relevant information, and to make recommendations as fits the case.

5. *Effective school districts extend school programs and services above and beyond their comprehensive curriculum offerings.* Extracurricular programs and student clubs are common in effective school programs. Attention is given to additional support services that are available to all students but especially important for some school districts in low-income areas.

Health services, vision and hearing testing, immunization programs and related extracurricular sports, dance, and even religious clubs are among the extended offering of high-quality school districts. We discussed the topic of prayer in schools in chapter 2. Prayer clubs sponsored by students have been ruled as being approved when such "clubs" are not sponsored or promoted by the school personnel. The literature is beginning to open the door once again to the concept of the community schools.

The Mott Foundation concept of community education has been on the table, although somewhat behind the scenes, for at least six decades. In short, community education addresses the concept that education's first and foremost purpose is to improve the community. Producing the knowledge and skills of students is one way to improve the community, as is improving the community's environment or improving the recreational/park facilities in the community.

We note the "new" emphasis on community education and its comprehensive coverage in two recent articles, "Inventing in What Works: Community Driven Strategies for Strong Public Schools in Georgia" (2015) and "Community Schools: Transforming Struggling Schools into Thriving Schools" (2016). We recommend the reading of these references for their ideas/recommendations regarding school improvement.

6. *Effective school programs are inclusive as revealed in their programs of service to all children and youth in the school community.* The topic of inclusiveness was detailed previously in chapter 2. Effective schools exemplify the educational concept of inclusiveness; the school's program is open and geared to all students in the community. Special needs students are welcomed, and their interests and special needs are professionally attended.

We consulted with a state department of education director and asked her about the primary controversies being faced by the department. Although we did not pursue further investigation of all of the issues being faced, the types of controversies named were somewhat surprising. Surprising not because the issues were not associated with education but because of the fact that the controversies actually were being attended by the state. The following list sets forth several controversial issues being encountered by educational departments at the state level, including the legislatures of the states:

- Complaints against school officials
- Student discipline
- Financial maleficence
- Teacher tenure
- Transportation disputes
- Negotiations agreements
- Residency
- Violation of school ethics
- Audit appeals
- Teacher retention rates
- Financing education
- Teacher development (support of new teachers)
- Anti-bullying measures
- Special education
- Overspent budgets
- Student residency
- Student discipline disputes
- Actions of local school boards
- Vocational education issues
- School finance issues
- The closing of schools due to inferior performance
- Competency-based educational performance
- Others

We have selected two additional controversial issues to discuss in this chapter: the controversial issues of *negotiation agreements* and *competency-based educational performance*.

THE CONTROVERSIAL EDUCATION ISSUE OF TEACHER NEGOTIATIONS: STATE LEVEL

Sawchuk (2011) underscored the changes and controversial issues surrounding the practice of collective bargaining. This author notes that the various states first made changes to compensation, then to evaluation systems, and then to tenure laws and then began to question collective bargaining and the status of teacher unionism. Some states introduced legislation to abolish collective bargaining. The underlying result centers on the gaining of decision-making powers for school boards and school administrators.

As would be expected, such moves are attacked by teachers' groups and controversy results.

Is politics involved in these deliberations? History serves to show that Democrats have traditionally supported collective bargaining, while Republicans have been opposed to the process. Similar to other political events, some states have changed from support to opposition as the state's governance administration changed. Sawchuk (2011) noted that several states have prohibited collective bargaining, several are considering doing so, and several continue to support it. Support and non-support continue to be present, and thus the controversies continue to flourish.

The Pros Regarding the Collective Bargaining Process in Education

- Collective bargaining increases the cooperation between teachers and the administrative personnel and school boards within the school district. Cooperation, rather than conflict, is needed for effective school operations.
- Collective negotiations protect teachers from the political changes that have a negative effect on the job.
- Collective negotiations give teachers a voice in the decisions made pertaining to their work in the school system.
- It serves to ensure that teachers' rights such as due process and teacher autonomy in the classroom are protected.
- It can result in an increase of teacher compensation and work environment improvements that serve to retain teachers in the profession.
- Increases in compensation and work conditions can, in turn, increase job satisfaction that results in increased productivity.
- Collective bargaining can be an open process and not one that is filled with under the table tactics.

The Cons Regarding the Collective Bargaining Process in Education

- Collective bargaining costs the taxpayers large sums of money.
- There is no end to collective bargaining. Once the matter of more compensation is approved, collective bargaining for additional fringe benefits, health insurance, work time, class size, leave provisions, travel expenses, and other benefits comes into play at the bargaining table.
- Bargaining results in having the teachers' association/union involved in every administrative decision and practice. Teacher evaluations, class size, work schedules, days for sick leave, workloads, school budgeting, duty-free lunches, teacher dismissal procedures, school program changes, and other

matters that are under the responsibility of the administration and school board are likely to be suggested for entry into the bargaining process.
- The time necessary to prepare for bargaining is time taken from student-centered program needs.
- All too often, the threat of teacher walkouts, work stoppages, picketing, teacher rallies, and actual strikes are always threatened and implemented. These actions are unfair to students who have come to school to learn.
- Member relationships are endangered by the conflicts that take place before, during, and after the process.
- Collective bargaining has three basic purposes. Teachers want more money, more benefits, and less work.

It is clear that the process of collective negotiations within the various states will continue to be up and down depending on the power structures within the school community and the political party in place. Nevertheless, at the time of this writing, the process of collective bargaining was under discussion in several states. For example, bills in some states have been introduced to bar bargaining by teachers' unions.

Cost appears to be a major concern. But cost does not appear to be the only reason for limiting collective bargaining. Such matters as teacher evaluation, class size, online learning, teacher tenure, and single salary schedules have entered the picture of things that are being brought to the negotiations table. Even the process of open or closed negotiations is among the items being placed on the bargaining table. The fact that the inhibiting of bargaining also increases problems for school boards and school administrators, and law makers tend to support it. That is, the disapproval of bargaining will lessen the power of the unions and leave other school personnel to carry the negative outcomes that result.

THE CONTROVERSIAL ISSUE OF COMPETENCY-BASED EDUCATIONAL PERFORMANCE

The practice of competency-based education (CBE) is both a state and local controversy. CBE is the practice of having high school students attend courses, do assignments, get credit, and eventually graduate based on what they know rather on the grade that they are in or how much time it took them to gain that level of knowledge and skill. Almost everyone has known a talented child that skipped a grade in elementary school; perhaps the child was moved from third grade to fourth grade after spending a short time in grade three. CBE is different, of course, since it commonly takes place in high school whereby the student takes a competency-based course and receives high school or even college credit for his or her successful performance.

The pluses and minuses of competency-based programs are considered as follows. We submit that the assessment of these factors serves a vital role in determining whether or not the student and the school personnel are prepared to gain in a positive way by initiating a program of CBE at the secondary school level.

The Pro Contentions in Favor of Competency-Based Education Programs

- A student can prove mastery of a certain required skill and then finish the course much sooner that in traditional systems. This fact allows the saving of both time and money.
- CBE is perfect for self-directed learners and especially those who need to balance school and other commitments.
- A student can determine how much time is needed to place on the course, get assessed, and then to move on.
- A student can determine his or her own schedule in relation to other commitments and interests.
- A faster high school graduation is possible. The student can graduate early and enter a field of work or enter college and finish earlier than is commonly possible.
- Education is much more affordable in competency-based programs.
- Teachers do a different job; much more coaching and mentoring is done. Less work is devoted to ongoing testing and grading homework papers.
- CBE can result in a much greater increase in the student's satisfaction for learning.
- CBE programs tend to contribute to a higher level of school graduation rates.
- The flexibility built into the program fits the needs of many students today.
- CBE students get far more control over their learning process.

The Con Contentions Related to Competency-Based Education Programs

- A key issue in competency-based programs in education is agreeing on what courses and skills the student should pursue.
- Trying to decide on the best methods to achieve the program's ends is most difficult.
- Attempting to track the student's progress in the competency-based program is difficult and ongoing.
- CBE programs must always comply with district/state standards. Keeping programs targeted on standards is difficult indeed.

- CBE programs call for many significant changes in teacher and school procedures. Time becomes a negative factor.
- Too many changes and challenges are encountered. Teacher turnover can leave the student at a loss.
- School personnel are not prepared to deal with the necessary changes and oversight needed in this program.
- Parents become suspicious and uncomfortable with their child being outside the regular classroom and away from classroom friends.
- For the program to be successful, a student must be a self-directed learner, and many students are not cut out for this arrangement.
- Many high school students do not have a clear idea as to what their future career might be. These kinds of thoughts tend to change during the school years. Choosing courses for such a student becomes guess work at best.
- Students must be prepared to work for as long as it takes for mastery. The assumption that every course will take less time than being in a regular classroom is not always the case.
- Most programs have a time frame in which the course must be assessed for mastery. A common rule is that the student has three times to test for mastery. If he or she does not meet the standard after three tries, they must throw in the towel.
- CBE is not for everyone. The student must have developed time management skills.
- Keeping track of the student's progress and giving feedback to the student has been found to be difficult.

So, what might your view on CBE? Are you on the pro side?

Perhaps the con side? Or are you undecided? Read the following section on the characteristics of personalized CBE and the seven design questions recommended by Marzano Research (2018). Doing so might be helpful to you in deciding your answer to the foregoing question.

Marzano Research on Competency-Based Education

Personalized CBE has:

- Students move on to the next level within a subject area only after they have demonstrated proficiency at the current level.
- The time required to learn content is not a factor in judging students' competencies.
- Students have multiple opportunities and ways to demonstrate proficiency with specific content.

- Development of student agency is a central focus in addition to proficiency with specific content.
- Students have a choice in the teaching and learning process.
- Students have voice in the teaching and learning process.

Marzano research suggests starting with seven design questions:

1. What content will be addressed within the system?
2. How will the learning environment support student learning?
3. How will instruction support student learning?
4. How will student proficiency be measured?
5. How will individual student needs and interests accommodate learning.
6. How will reporting facilitate student learning?
7. How do we transition to a personalized competency-based education (PCBE) system?

In this chapter, the focus has been on the controversial education issues and related debates at the state level. As noted at the outset of the chapter, almost every state controversy/issue has a close relationship with the same issue at the local school level. For example, the controversies of teacher tenure, financing education, special education, teacher tenure, and many others have similar debates. In the final chapter of the book, the educational controversies at the national level are addressed.

Key Chapter Ideas and Recommendations

- Educational controversies at the local school level most often are also identified with controversies taking place at the state level. However, a reduction of controversy at one or the other of these program levels does not mean that the issue has been resolved at both levels of authority.
- The selection of local school controversies at the state level seemingly is unending as well. Many state educational debates have historical connections, and others tend to change on and off depending on the changes that take place in the nation and within state and national governments.
- The pro and con arguments for or against a state educational controversy are such that a best solution might be reached until the next political power structure takes office.
- In some cases, state educational controversies reach the highest court in the land. However, the court's ruling may lessen the turmoil surrounding the issue but the controversy remains in voice.
- The characteristics of effective school districts have been identified. Achieving these ends in all schools within the state, however, has been most difficult. Wide disparities in property values and taxable income are common in almost every state in the land.

- The matter of local control is a controversy of the times. School boards are losing out to state mandates and to their own "loss of leadership" problems, including policy development.
- Community education in America once again has raised its voice in relation to being a solution for school inclusiveness and school community improvement.
- State educational controversial issues are extensive. The state's focus as a service agency for local schools has changed over the past several years and presently has become much more of an oversight control agency.
- Collective bargaining has been in and out of major controversy. At present, the force is against collective bargaining, and several states have or plan to have legislative bills that stop the process or greatly detail the agenda items that can be negotiated.
- Pro and con arguments related to controversial matters in education are useful in gaining an understanding of the problems that must be attended. However, solutions for resolving the differences are not readily established or implemented.
- The compensation of teachers will continue to be discussed and debated. As long as the public schools are supported by public tax funds, education will remain as one member of the political web that exists and competes for the state's resources. Politics is not only present in almost every compensation debate, but it is also among the primary reasons why the debates are taking place.
- Competency-based education programs look much like efforts to resolve the problems related to unsatisfactory programs. However, the con arguments for the closing of such programs commonly reveal additional controversial debates.

Discussion Questions

1. Consider one or two of the controversial issues facing state education legislatures and departments. Use your magic wand to suggest changes that must be made to resolve and implement changes based on your recommended selections.
2. Suppose that you have been asked to speak to a state committee that is considering the matter of competency-based education. List three recommendations that you would suggest. For example, what key suggestions might you have regarding the state controversy of collective bargaining?
3. The controversy of teacher tenure has been an historical matter for state education departments. What steps might you suggest for resolving the controversies surrounding this issue? For example, would you speak positively for the right of teachers to bargain for compensation improvements or for leaving compensation matters to the states for equity reasons?

4. Assume that the matter of school takeovers by the state has become a major controversial issue within your school community. One of Wymore high schools has been rated as underperforming and is likely to be taken over by the state. As the current president of the Wymore School District, how might you address this action at a forthcoming school board meeting? Avoid comments relative to just investigating the matter additionally or seeking more information. Instead, consider the school board's responsibility of policy development and the accountabilities implied by the purposes set forth for establishing an effective academic program in each school within the school district.
5. Review the pros and cons related to the matter of disbanding state departments of education and then set forth your opinions on this controversial issue. Keep in mind that the question focuses on state departments of education and state legislature will continue to exist. Finally, give *your* reasons for or against the move of disbanding state departments of education.

Case Study: The Behind-the-Scenes Campaign

The Golden Globe Institute reportedly was a nonprofit organization that operated on the motto of "Inclusiveness Is Our Motto; Opportunities Is Our Promise." The institute was owned and operated by a wealthy business man in the Wymore School District. The institute was receiving monetary support from the state on the bases that it was serving children and youth with special needs that were not being met under the local public schools. Students with special needs were welcomed in the institute's program.

Effective lobbying by the owner of the institute and other Wymore supporters who had given generously to recently elected state legislators gained the approval of the state legislature to award state funding comparable to that of regular financial support of local public schools in the school district. Over time, with the state financial support and tuition fees, the institute became a profitable enterprise. The owner's annual salary was reported as being over $1 million.

Oversight of charter schools in the state did require budget reports, but the Golden Globe Institute did not do so on the basis that it included a special program emphasis for special needs students and therefore was not a charter school as defined by law. An investigation of the institute's expenditures revealed that monies given to the program were being mixed with general funds from tuition fees, contributions, and funds by other supporters that were not identified in any institute reports. Controversies became prevalent on the fact that the institute's financial dealings were not being accounted for in the same way that local public schools were required to do. Various members of the state legislature voiced support of the institute's financial procedures.

The institute readily reported on its major achievements and especially the high academic results of the internal testing program. Objective results of the institute's testing program were not readily available. Other information related to the actual school enrolment figures, enrollment requirements, information on the nature of students being enrolled, number of special needs students, or the qualifications and salaries for the institute personnel, or the CEO and school's institute committee was not made available.

Discussion Questions

The name of the Golden Globe Institute and all of the personnel and information are fictitious. The politics, relationships, and budget figures are manufactured as well. The case is stated as set forth earlier for the purpose of noting the general state problems that have been encountered in various state education departments. Without question, the controversies related to charter schools and other private school programs are indeed evidenced in contemporary state education programs.

1. In your opinion, should a charter, private, or parochial school be operated outside the jurisdiction of the state? State your opinion with appropriate rationale.
2. The case study raises the question as to what extent any K–12 education program should be under the jurisdiction of the state. For example, should such a decision of control be left to the decision of parents or to other local agencies in the school district in our democratic society?
3. What factors of our time have contributed to the expanding procedure of choice related to the education of children and youth?
4. What do local politics have to do with the answers to questions of education control by the state government? How does politics enter the control question of education within the state?

REFERENCES

Brush, Katelyn. (2016, July 13). Vocational education from the 1900s to today. blog.studentcaffe.com/vocational-education-1900s-today/.

Carter, C. (no date). The case against standardized tests. From the web: testcritic.homestead.com/files/standardized-tests.html.

Dingerson, Leigh (2015). Investing in what works: Community-Driven strategies for strong public schools in Georgia (2015). https://eric.gov?id=ED585793.

Frankl, Evie (2016). Community schools: Transforming struggling schools into thriving schools. Southern Education Foundation. https://eric.ed.gov?id=ED5858772.

Goldstein, D. (2012, April 19). The future of vocational education. *The Nation.* https://www.the nation.com/article/future-vocational-education/.

Gross, S. M. (2011, December 12). *Pros and cons of a mayoral takeover of schools.* From the web: https://www.kcur.org/post/pros-and-cons-mayor-takeover-schools#stream/0.

Marzano Research (2018). *Competency-based education.* https:/www.Marzanoresearch.com/personalized-competency-education-1.

Mathis, M. (2009–2018). Teacher tenure debate: Pros and cons. *Teach Hub-K-12, New Lessons and Shared Resources by Teachers and for Teachers.* www.teachhub.com/teacher-tenure-pros-cons.

Norton, M. S. (2015). *The changing landscape of school leadership: Recalibrating the school principalship.* Lanham, MD: Rowman & Littlefield.

Pennington, K. (2014, June 5). How state takeover school districts shake up teacher professional development. *Education K-12.* Center for American Progress, Washington, D.C.

Rosen, P. (2014–2018). Special education: Federal law vs. state law. *Understood, Free and Appropriate Public Education, IDEA.* New York, NY: Understood Education.

Sawchuk, S. (2011, February 7). States aim to curb collective bargaining. *Education Week, SPOTLIGHT,* 30 (20), 1, 20. Bethesda, MD: Educational Projects in Education.

Schnell, L. (2018, December 4). Teachers top the class of lawmakers: Election winners carry their concerns from the classroom. *Arizona Republic Newspaper, USA Today,* Section B.

Timar, T. B. (1997). The institutional role of state education departments: A historical perspective. *American Journal of Education,* 105 (3), 231–60.

Chapter 4

Educational Controversies at the Federal Level

Primary Chapter Goal: To identify selected educational controversies that center at the federal government level and to present the pros and cons of the education debates along with available information related to each controversial selection.

Many of the contemporary educational controversies at the federal level have had long histories. Thus, a summary of the history of education in relation to legislative action at the federal level serves to give us a better understanding of the more recent controversies. The changes have taken place relative to the U.S. Department of Education, Common Core, No Child Left Behind, local control of education, school choice, and other programs are examples of the ins and outs and ups and downs of federal educational debates.

The concept that education is a national concern is not as appropriate today as in previous years. Local school systems are under pressure from both the state and federal governments to function according to imposed standards or be placed on probation or lose monetary support needed for program support. The matter of having a national curriculum has come into play led by the entry of the Common Core requirements established during the Obama administration. School governance has been greatly influenced by the increasing involvement of federal government in local school affairs. School superintendents commonly name complying with external mandates as one of the ten leading problems facing them.

A BRIEF HISTORY OF EDUCATIONAL LEGISLATION AND PROGRAM ACTIVITIES AT THE FEDERAL LEVEL

The Continental Congress was an assembly of delegates from the 13 colonies, which became the governing body during the Revolutionary War. Major educational steps taken by the Congress were addressed in the passing of the Land Ordinance of 1785 and later the Northwest Land Ordinance of 1787 drafted by Thomas Jefferson. The Land Ordinance declared that the No. 16 lot of every township be reserved for the maintenance of public schools, which served as a significant thrust for public education and the future of the republic.

The Land Ordinance of 1785 focused on making public education a requirement within each township. There was the objective of wanting all children to become good citizens, but also there was a need for educating the young people for roles as ministers, priests, and capable office holders (Norton, 2018). Following the era of colonization, settlement during the early years of 1620 to 1763, eras of American Revolution and the New Nation, the national expansion and reconstruction, and the Progressive Era were experienced in America. It is noted that the federal government was mainly responsible for creating a public school for all children, and this model served well for expanding education in a growing territory toward the West.

Cook and Klay (2014) underscored the fact that George Washington was adamant about establishing a plan for universal education in the United States. Washington argued that an educated citizenry was essential for able participation in a democratic government. This contention has been reiterated by many presidents who have served the nation throughout its history. The question about who should be included in this "universal" education was not always clear. Did it include the black citizens, female citizens, and other less-fortunate persons in the nation?

John Adams, America's second president, was clear in setting forth his primary views on the importance of free public education for all the people. President Adams contended that liberty could not be preserved without a general knowledge among the people. Education was not only for the rich and noble, but it must also become a national concern that is financially supported by the nation's citizenry.

Thomas Jefferson is noted especially for his lifetime contributions to our country and to the importance of public education in America. In his letters to Washington and to John Adams, Jefferson expressed the hope that public schools would become the keystone in the arch of the government. Interestingly enough, Jefferson did not favor education being controlled by the federal or state governments. Rather, he was of the opinion that the local school district and its parents were best suited to control the common school. Any centralized control was objectionable in the view of Jefferson. Agreement on Jefferson's views was not unanimous.

A comprehensive review of the contributions of the nation's 44 presidents is beyond the scope of this chapter. However, the reader is advised of the recent book on the topic of U.S. presidents' views and significant educational contributions published by Rowman & Littlefield in 2018. The publication is titled *The Whitehouse and Education through the Years*. The educational legacies of each of the nation's 44 presidents from George Washington to Donald Trump are included in the book.

For the purpose of showing the various educational issues associated with elected national presidents, a brief report of selected relevant program efforts is presented in the following section. The reader will readily see the ongoing controversies that have historically accompanied changing political administrations in America. The many federal educational controversies and related debates of the Congress, the up and downs of the U.S. Department of Education, and other government agencies are then detailed in other sections of the chapter.

DEBATES AND CONTROVERSIES OF PRESIDENTIAL ORIGIN

George Washington (1789–1797)—Washington was adamant about establishing a plan for universal education in the United States for all citizens. (Controversy)—Is it necessary that all children and youth be educated? Does the plan include children of the black population? Does it include the female population?

John Adams (1797–1801)—Adams was adamant in his promotion of education for all citizens. (Controversy)—Some persons contended that he was referring only to Caucasians rather than black people.

Thomas Jefferson (1801–1809)—Jefferson was a strong supporter of the common school. He was hopeful that his idea of a public school would become the keystone in the arch of our government. (Controversy)—Any centralized control by the state was objectionable to the views of Jefferson. Others strongly favored state or federal control. Some parents did not want their children to attend a common school.

Abraham Lincoln (1861–1865)—One of the most significant educational acts of the time was the Morrill Act that was also known as the Land Grant College Act. Although the Morrill Act focused on higher education, its impact on public school programming was significant. (Controversy)—It was first assumed that the applicants for the nearly free territory would be all white. This certainly was not the case. Applications included African

Americans, single women, and poor families. Major controversies took place in the fact that the railroads, which owned most of the territory, fought the land grants. Due to the fact that many new landowners were not knowledgeable or skilled in farming, land failures occurred and many persons left the land after filing bankruptcy.

Andrew Johnson (1865–1869)—An historic initiative performed by President Johnson was that of his signing the first Department of Education legislation. (Controversy)—Much concern was expressed relative to federal department's control within the states. Since that time, federal control of education has been a topic of debate. The status of the Department of Education historically has been established, disestablished, and reopened once again.

Theodore Roosevelt (1901–1909)—The Smith-Lever Act of 1914 was enacted that led to the development of extended programs of agriculture education, extension courses, and a new emphasis on home economics and agriculture programs in public school curricular programs. (Controversy)—Since farming was a major occupation during this era, more pros than cons were bent upon the agricultural legislation. Teacher preparation was among the most pressing issues. There were questions regarding the financial support for the programs at the local level as agricultural programs spread to the city as well.

Woodrow Wilson (1913–1921)—The Smith-Hughes Act of 1917 was significantly added to the focus on vocational education at the public school level. Local public school programs included agriculture, home economics, and the industrial trades. (Controversy)—Debates took place, however, as to where such programs should take place. Concerns included the fact that the program took students away from the traditional school campus and how the program was to be interpreted for female students. In addition, how were the students for the program to be identified and should female students be prepared to assume work in agriculture-related careers as millinery and garment work were debated?

Herbert Hoover (1929–1933)—Hoover's most significant leadership contribution for children was his work as cofounder of the United Nations Children's Fund (UNICEF), which worked for children around the world in the area of health, welfare, and rights. (Controversy)—Concern was expressed in some quarters regarding Hoover's placing of his time and effort on UNICEF rather than on the much more important factors related to the deep depression that took place primarily during the years 1929–1933.

Franklin D. Roosevelt (1933–1945)—Roosevelt would head the list of presidents that instituted the most education and education-related programs in the United States. During his administration the Civilian Conservation Corps (CCC), the Works Administration Program (WAP), the GI Bill, the National Youth Administration (NYA), the Federal Emergency Relief

Administration (FERA), the Emergency Education Program (EEP), and other New Deal policies all had major influence on public education. (Controversy)—Among the various program controversies was that of the NYA program that was placed in the U.S. Office of Education and directed by Secretary Studebaker. Further problems resulted when the program was placed under Harry Hopkins, director of WPA. The National Education Association strongly objected. FDR explained that the National Education and the NYA programs were to provide relief to youth and that another person under Hopkins was more experienced to administer the NYA program.

Reportedly, Roosevelt had certain problems regarding his opinion that public school personnel did not want to make changes that were necessary for improving education in America. A study by Dass (2014) did show evidence that public schools were not sufficiently supported by FDR. Roosevelt's opinions about public school education evolved from his belief that public schools were not meeting the needs of the nation's students from low-income families.

Harry S. Truman (1945–1953)—Educational contributions by Truman included such provisions as federal aid and the appointment of the Presidential Committee on Civil Rights that focused on equal rights for black children educationally. (Controversy)—Truman's educational contributions led to later actions by the Committee on Civil Rights that focused on equal rights for black children. Most citizens are aware of the many troubled debates that accompanied actions related to rights for all children and youth, including the later court case of *Brown v. Board of Education of Topek* in 1954. The Supreme Court of the United States ruled that segregated schools were "inherently unequal," and this fact violated black rights under the Fourteenth Amendment to the U.S. Constitution.

Dwight D. Eisenhower (1953–1961)—Eisenhower's National Defense Education Act of 1957 (NDEA) was one of the four major happenings of education-related programs during his administration. (Controversy)—The passing of the NDEA was predicated on the belief that education programs were falling behind Russia, Japan, and other foreign nations. Our students were not sufficiently capable in the areas of mathematics, the sciences, and foreign language subjects. Several publications focused serious attention on the failures of public schools in America, including the 1953 book by Bestor titled *Educational Wastelands,* and Rickover's book *Education and Freedom,* published in 1959. Controversies relating to the need for improved teaching in the academic subjects occurred resulting in the reduction of courses in the fine arts and social sciences.

John F. Kennedy (1961–1963)—Kennedy's push for improving the health and physical conditioning of children and youth was one program that was widely established in local schools during his relatively short term in office, but the program seemed to phase out of most school education programs after his untimely death. With the exception, perhaps, that more time on physical education activities took away from time on other subjects, no major controversies were prevalent.

This comment is not meant to infer that Kennedy was not especially concerned about K–12 program's emphasis on the academics because not only the academic subjects of math, science, and foreign language loomed important during his administration, but special education, vocational education, and English were emphasized in his messages to Congress and the public as well. Controversy—Although the nation was tuned into the need for public school improvements for meeting the growing threats posed by Russia, other subjects in the fine arts were often reduced or even eliminated. The everlasting controversy of local control also came into play.

Lyndon B. Johnson (1963–1969)—The federal budget for education virtually tripled during Johnson's term in office. The Elementary and Secondary Education Act passed during his administration represented the federal government's deepest plunge into the operations of local and state educational governance. (Controversy)—The primary debates resulting from the Elementary and Secondary Education Act centered on the concern of federal control of education. Federal monetary support also found its way into parochial schools, and wonderment about whether federal funds would be available for increasing teachers' salaries entered into education debates as well.

Jimmy Carter (1977–1981)—Carter made several important contributions to public school education, including vocational education, free kindergarten, and funding support for children with disability. Carter worked toward the establishment of the department of education at the federal level. (Controversy)—Carter's support of public monies for parochial schools was a problem in many quarters. Carter's strong belief in the separation of church and state did result in causing some upsets among religious groups.

Ronald Reagan (1981–1989)—Controversial issues facing Reagan during his term of office included his back-and-forth position on the existence of the Department of Education, his interest in reconstituting prayer in schools, and the use of standardized student testing as being the answer to local school accountability. Reagan's statement that the schools didn't need more funding and that what they needed was tougher standards caused much concern on the part of educators and others. (Controversy)—Along with the foregoing controversies, Reagan wanted to give tax credits for those families who wanted to send their children to private schools. In addition, his view regarding higher pay for teachers included the concept of basing such decisions on teacher performance. This concept raised complaints from teachers' associations nationally.

George H. W. Bush (1989–1993)—Although George H. W. Bush wanted to be known as the education president, it is rather difficult to find specific educational contributions that took place during H. W. Bush's administration, although he did have a program called America 2000k. Nothing much appears to have come of it. (Controversy)—Bush expressed his concern related to the education bureaucracy that was controlling everything. The bureaucracy was the teachers' unions that took the control from local schools whereby teachers and not parents were in control of education.

William J. Clinton (1993–2001)—Clinton wanted schools to change so that accountability measures could be implemented that required the states and school districts to turn around failing schools or close them. (Controversy)—One can see the controversy that was conjured up by this contention of federal control. In addition, Clinton wanted subject matter and skill tests for new teachers. "What works, and we know what works will be supported by federal funding," stated Clinton.

Barack Obama (2001–2009)—Barack Obama's administration was deeply involved in public school and charter school education programs. The programs No Child Left Behind, Race to the Top, and Common Core each had a full history of debates. (Controversy)—Major debates and resentment were directed toward the Common Core mandates. Both courses and course requirements for instruction in the local classrooms of the nation were set forth in this legislation. Both teacher and administrator resentment was prevalent nationally.

During the 2016 presidential campaign that ultimately ended with Donald Trump as president, Trump and other candidates stated that, if elected to the presidency, Common Core would be disbanded. Since Trump became president, hundreds of school districts have dropped the Common Core requirements although its remnants still are being practiced in many school districts today. At the time of this writing, America was waiting to see just what the federal government would "mandate" for public school operations. School choice and charter schools were at the top of the agenda within the U.S. Department of Education.

THE UNENDING LISTINGS OF EDUCATIONAL CONTROVERSIES AT THE FEDERAL LEVEL

The listing of controversial issues in education within the United States is virtually unending. The debates on education at the federal level range from the contents of textbooks to the issues of sex education, racial discrimination, prayer, teacher assessment and evaluation, gun control, teachers' unions, bilingual education, corporal punishment, and many other controversial issues. We have selected several burning controversies for discussion in this chapter, which include school choice and charter schools, racial discrimination, banning of textbooks, curricular involvement, local control, national education standards, social programs, and redshirting.

Other controversial issues such as school prayer, high-stakes testing, sex education, online education, student grading, bilingual education, and others have been considered in earlier chapters of the book. We repeat the fact that almost every one of the educational controversies being encountered in education has major implications for the programs at the local, state, and federal levels of government.

THE CONTROVERSIES OF SCHOOL CHOICE AND CHARTER SCHOOLS AT THE FEDERAL LEVEL

In an effort to determine the major educational controversies at the federal level, the realization that federal education issues are inextricably related to local and state educational issues must be kept in mind. For example, the federal education issues of funding, gun control, racial discrimination, unions, praying in schools, social programs, federal control, student busing, academic achievement, charter schools, and school vouchers also are relevant controversies at the state and local levels. The first federal controversy being discussed in this chapter is school choice and vouchers.

THE CONTROVERSY OF SCHOOL CHOICE AND VOUCHERS AT THE FEDERAL LEVEL

School choice is the primary educational issue being promoted presently at the federal level. In one recent national survey, school vouchers received a "pro" response by 65 percent of the study participants. It follows that the controversy for this issue centers on the fact that another 35 percent of the participants were against the voucher concept. The "voucher concept" constitutes the procedure of giving parents a "certificate" that is used for tuition to any parochial or private schools within the region. The funds are taken from the state taxes, and the voucher commonly does not cover the full tuition fees. As a result of state funding for school choice, education funds for the state's local public schools obviously are decreased.

At the time of this writing, the matter of what would be done at the federal level in regard to school choice, charter schools, for-profit corporation schools, and other forms of education had yet to be announced. Various pronouncements regarding what direction the Trump administration, alongside

Betsey DeVos' leadership of the Department of Education, would take were not completely clear. It has been said that the present administration might favor a savings account system for families. Reportedly, families could use these savings to attend any kind of school so desired, including a regular public school. Some persons have expressed the belief that such a savings program would reduce or actually prohibit continuing controversy on the subject of federal support for education. We believe otherwise.

The Pros in Support of the School Choice Concept and School Vouchers

- The majority of the nation's citizens appear to be in favor of school choice using the voucher method for school funding.
- School choice supports parents' rights to choose their children's education setting.
- School choice gives the bests schools to lure the best students within the region.
- Charter schools represent a way to teach specific subjects outside the public school system.
- By allowing parents to choose a private school, parents no longer have to pay for public education that they do not use.
- At present, many students are locked into failing schools. School choice opens the doors to many other educational opportunities.
- School choice is the American way.
- School choice serves to reduce and even eliminate controversy. Parents make the choice of which schools to attend, not the state or other governance bodies.
- Choice is not necessarily a one-way street. If the parents and child do not like their first choice for schooling, there is an opportunity to make a more favorable choice.
- School choice can result in reducing controversy. Private schools that are based on a religious foundation, for example, can have prayer in schools and so the provision serves as a solution to prayer as a major issue in public school today.
- "Let's use the education dollars to follow the child instead of forcing the child to follow the dollars" (contributed to Education Secretary Betsy DeVos).

The Cons Opposing the School Choice Concept and Charter Schools

- The concept that local public schools should be locally funded and controlled is an American concept historically.
- The idea that public funds are used to support private schools is outside the concept of separation of church and state.

- Public schools in American already are unfunded. School vouchers for school choice undermine the ability to provide students a comprehensive education.
- The concept of giving tax credits toward the support of private schools means that many taxpayers are giving their funds to a cause that they do not support.
- Charter schools do not have to account for the tax dollars that they spend.
- There is no research that charter and private schools increase the scholarly abilities of students.
- The failure of charter schools in America is a growing statistic.
- Parents who chose private schools lose out regarding the way a child is educated. Churches, for example, do have their own philosophies as to what to teach.
- The approval of charter schools and other schools of choice damages many public schools that are already in need of additional financial support.
- Charter schools today are found to be closed in many ways, including financial accountability, information concerning teacher, administrator, and owner salaries.
- Students who live in poverty have problems entering charter schools in many states. Early reports indicate that such students have difficulty being accepted into a charter school. If they are accepted for enrollment, they do not do well in the school's learning program.
- The record reveals that many students are dropping from charter schools and that many charter and private schools are closing and leaving students in the lurch.
- Vouchers are a threat to the nation's public school system.

Many charter schools, private schools, religious schools, and other school options are without highly qualified personnel to teach and administer quality programs. Lay boards commonly have not consisted of members with education/business knowledge required in such roles. Too many reports of fraudulent business practices and failing educational programs have been present in the absence of effective program standards and questionable financial dealings. The problem of the lack of transparency in the way in which financial matters are handled in charter schools is expressed on the part of those persons who oppose school choice and charter program operations.

There has been some major shifting on the support of charter schools as reported by Sally Ho of the Associated Press (2018). Ho's article serves to point out the primary controversies surrounding to school choice and charter schools. For example, several states have elected new state officials who reportedly are more skeptical of charter schools than their election opponents. Election winners have been openly in favor of supporting more accountability and more consideration for halting of the for-profit schools in the various states. Newly elected governors in several states have expressed their reservations about the growth of charter schools and, in turn, are expressing more support for the traditional public schools that are serving the large majority of students in the nation.

School choice does not mean that any group of individuals can agree to establish a school and administer it according to the quality of learning needed in our democratic society. If mediocrity is accepted, then our democratic republic is endangered. As many of our national leaders have voiced, "A democratic nation cannot be sustained without an educated citizenry."

It seems important that we keep a ready look on what comes to the legislative floor regarding federal financial support. One might not find the word "vouchers" used in further announcements. The term *vouchers* conjures up controversy and debates. As has been stated in some reports, the words *blended learning, innovation, finding solutions,* and *reimagining education* might come up as a cover for the term *vouchers* in future discussions.

THE CONTROVERSY OF PUBLIC SCHOOL FUNDING AT THE FEDERAL LEVEL

The federal government currently is supporting public school education with an approximate expenditure of $1.15 billion annually, which represents approximately 8 percent of public school financial support. Thus, the local school districts and the respective states pay the other 92 percent of America's public school financial support. In view of the relatively low level of federal support, wherein lies the controversy? The controversy lies somewhere among the beliefs such as the federal government is not paying enough attention to support public education, it is paying too much attention, it should be paying more, and it should not be paying anything. The latter contention centers on the opinion that the federal government should keep its hands out of education at the local level.

So far in the Trump administration, it is quite clear that its direction relative to K–12 education in the United States centers on school choice. The school choice and charter school programs received the lion's share of education support. For example, Trump's K–12 budget increased charter school spending by $168 million. The 2018 budget created new private school choice programs with $250 million. The budget included $1 billion to encourage school districts to allow federal dollars meant for low-income students to follow those students to public schools of their choice.

We need not list the pros and cons of school choice and charter school funding, since this was accomplished previously in this chapter. The information as to "if and how" the foregoing budget provisions have led to reductions in regular public school programs is not clear at this time. However, the last con statement in the foregoing section related to school choice and charter schools stated that "vouchers are a threat to public school education." However, as noted by staff writer Ho (2018, December 9), teachers unions are among the critics that reject charters as drains on the cash-starved public schools. At this time, however, the major push for school choice and charter schools by the Department of Education in the Trump administration is in full support of charter schools as revealed in both party actions and budget allocations.

THE BANNING OF BOOKS CONTROVERSY

The matter of book banning in public schools is an ongoing controversy nationally. The two sides of the book-banning debate tend to focus on: (1) parents have a right to decide what material their children are exposed to, and (2) parents may control what their own children read but not to restrict what books are available to others. Butler University Libraries and Center for Academic Technology (2017, September 11) used the source of Fort Lewis College to identify the nine primary reasons for the banning of books. These nine reasons are summarized as follows:

1. *Racial issues:* about or encouraging racism toward one or more groups of people.
2. *Encouragement of "damaging lifestyles":* content encourages lifestyle choices that are not of the norm or could be considered dangerous or damaging.
3. *Blasphemous dialog:* uses words viewed as profane or swearing that are commonly viewed as offensive.
4. *Sexual situations or dialog:* content includes sex that is viewed as inappropriate.
5. *Violence or negativity:* contains violence or too negative or depressing.
6. *Presence of witchcraft:* magic or witchcraft themes are often objectionable.
7. *Religious affiliations:* contains religious information viewed as being unpopular or are not in place of those in the public view.
8. *Political bias:* contains content that is viewed as being a political extreme such as communism.

9. *Age inappropriateness:* The book's content is viewed as being inappropriate for the age level for which it is directed. Sex is the most common topic on which school books are banned. Other common book-banning topics center on evolution, creationism, and intelligent design.

The Pros and Cons of the Banning of Books in School Courses and Libraries

The Pros for Banning Certain School Books

- Some books have explicit words and illustrations that are vulgar and violent. Therefore, they are inappropriate for certain levels of children in the school.
- Parents have the right to decide what material that their children are exposed to and when.
- Some inappropriate school books have information that encourages causal sex at an earlier age.
- Some books focus on topics of murder, death, religion, suicide, sex, peer pressure, and others that are very controversial.
- Banning prevents children from reading books that are inappropriate for their age.
- Banning prevents the putting of bad ideas into the minds of vulnerable children.
- Pornographic material has no place in the school's classroom or library.
- Too many books today focus on subjects such as religion, race, sex, lifestyles, and politics that are not appropriate for the child's age level.

The Cons for Not Banning Certain School Books

- Opting one's child out of reading certain books is no protection. Children are surrounded by other sources and persons who read and know a book's content. The "words" get around in any case and mostly from undesirable sources.
- Parents may control what their own child reads but cannot restrict what books are available to others.
- Books focus on the world of living. Banned books are among those books essential for cultural development.
- Books are portal to different experiences, and reading encourages empathy and social-emotional development.
- Book banning violates students' First Amendment rights.
- The reading of different books allows the child to learn about things and places he or she may never get to see or know.
- For one thing, a list of banned books included the Holy Bible as #6.

- Books are an outset for learning. The child's vocabulary is not only increased, but reading also lends to the improvement of the use of the English language.
- Book reading of all kinds serves to help people think, question, and explore.
- Book reading allows for people to see the pros and cons of ideas and opinions and to make up one's own mind as to what to accept.
- The banning of a book in a school most likely will just encourage the child to locate the book elsewhere since it must have content of real interest.
- It should not be up to the state or school authorities to decide what is right or wrong for students to read. It's like having the grocery store manager put on the shelves what he believes everyone should eat.
- Banning books in school violates the freedoms that Americans are supposed to have automatically with the obtaining of citizenship.
- By banning books from schools, we prevent our students from learning about controversial topics in a safe environment.
- Books must not be banned because just one parent challenges the work. An overall parental decision on such matters is a major factor of what is meant by local control of education and the school curriculum.
- School boards and professional teachers have a responsibility for protecting the minds of students and covering age material.

Book banning nationally does have an historical record. Since its establishment in 1982, Banned Books Week (Leigh, 2014) has recorded 11,000 books as being challenged. Being challenged does not mean that the book was banned since most challenges don't result in banishment. When they do get banned, they do so for good reasons. Some are challenged for strange reasons. Reportedly, *The Wonderful World of OZ* was challenged at an elementary school since it was accused of encouraging children to break dishes so they would not have to dry them. In another strange case, *My Friend Flicka* was challenged because a female dog was referred to as a "bitch."

The question must be asked regarding just how parents are to "protect" students from reading certain books. Books in bookstores, libraries, on the web, told in the movies, or in the hands of another student are extremely likely to get into the hands of the student. We contend that a "controversial" book might be best in the hands of a qualified teacher. By this comment, we mean that the necessary content and language used would be explained best by a knowledgeable English teacher or some parents would be able to discuss the book's content as well.

One senior student told of the book *The Fall of the House of Usher*. The student and the class read the book as a horror story. He learned much later in life that the book was a story of incest. He expressed the belief that he could have "handled" the real story and benefited by its contents more fully. The argument that such a book should not be in the classroom in the first place is countered by pointing out that the book would be easily available to the student from far, less-controlled sources. Of course, we are merely underscoring the controversies surrounding the banning of books in K–12 schools.

THE CONTROVERSY OF THE FEDERAL GOVERNMENT'S CURRICULAR INVOLVEMENT IN EDUCATION

The controversies of student achievement have been onboard for several decades. The focus within the controversy, however, has taken different turns. That is, several years ago vocational education was part of the federal debates. The lack of student physical fitness, low student academic achievement, special education, vocational education, and special education have been emphasized by federal agencies at different times. Common Core took over the emphasis by the federal government for several years until school choice and charter schools took over educational debates when Donald Trump's administration entered the scene.

Comparing education budgets from one presidential administration to another is difficult. According to our best calculations, the education budget of Donald Trump is approximately $59 billion. Barack Obama's education budget was approximately $46.7 billion, and George W. Bush's education budget was approximately $53.1 billion. The controversies over to Donald Trump's education budget rest in its large expenditures for school choice and charter schools. Considerable difficulty lies in knowing just what the education budgets do cover. For example, do the budgets include only K–12 education, or do they include higher education and other education expenditures such as student loans and parts of vocational program expenses?

In America, citizens have some say as to whom they want to represent in matters that pertain to living in a democratic nation. In the same way, local control of schools demands the control of educational matters by professionals who serve toward the best interests of all students. School boards are the ultimate local bodies that determine policy matters for school purposes. We contend that the school curriculum should be determined in broad policy statements by state legislatures.

In turn, local school boards determine the school district's policies that meet the state purposes and bend toward the views of the local citizenry as represented by the local school board. How the school board's list of goals and objectives is implemented is the decision of local school administrators and professional staff. The responsibilities of curricular offerings and book resources should rest with the local professional members of the school district.

In the following section we set forth several pros and cons that are commonly stated for and against the federal involvement in education at the local school level. We do make note, however, that the similar topic of national standards was discussed in detail in chapter 2. Thus, the pros and cons on these matters tend to be quite similar.

The Pros and Cons of Federal Involvement/Control of Local School Education

The Pros in Support of Federal Involvement/Control of Local School Education

- The U.S. Constitution includes the purposes of the federal government, including forming a more perfect Union, establishing justice, promoting the general welfare, and securing the blessings of liberty to ourselves and our prosperity. When important matters such as the education of our citizenry and the need go beyond the ability of the states, then the federal government must assume the responsibility for meeting the foregoing purposes.
- Students have been ill-served by local school education programs that differ widely among the 50 states. Such negative results must be attended by a higher level of government.
- States and local school districts have made mistakes, and some have ill-served students due to regional incompetence and ineffective leadership. Federal attention has become essential.
- The importance of an educated citizenry to sustain a democratic republic is reason enough for the federal government to be directly involved in America's education programs.
- What is needed is to eliminate many of the unproductive education offices at the state and county levels that replicate what is being done elsewhere. Such a reduction would move more resources to the federal level for promoting educational services.
- When states lack the resources to successfully manage their own internal education systems, then it is time to move the responsibilities to the federal level for the improvement of education nationally.

The Cons of Not Supporting the Federal Control of Education

- There has been no research or empirical evidence that federal involvement will improve student learning. More federal involvement does not guarantee higher-quality education.

- Federal control/involvement in local school education is not to be instituted in local school programs for one best reason: it is unconstitutional.
- Attempting to administer local school education programs from offices in Washington, D.C., is ludicrous. If a primary purpose of education is to meet the interests and needs of the individual student, how well can this purpose be met by some persons or offices at the national level?
- Local schools continue to be confused by the mandates that the federal government has set upon schools at the local level. Common Core, No Child Left Behind, and other costly federal education programs have failed, and others are destined to meet the same fate.
- Political administration historically changes, and with each change comes a change in what education must become. This on-and-off switch leaves local schools unable to gain stability in an education program that meets the real needs of students.
- Presidents throughout history have stood for the principle of local control of school programs. Thomas Jefferson did not favor education being controlled by the state or federal government.
- Look at what's really resulted from the millions of dollars spent on federal education programs. Where are the positive results? Let's just give that money to the local school district where the real needs of children and youth can be best attended.

THE EDUCATIONAL CONTROVERSIES RELATIVE TO NATIONAL EDUCATION STANDARDS

The national standards for education serve as guidelines for teaching the content of curricula in the primary and secondary schools. The national standards establish what is to be taught in schools along with standardized tests to measure if the required learning standards were achieved. The establishment of the national education standards has been a debated subject for several decades. The controversial history of the national standards requirements is lengthy and beyond the scope of this chapter. However, the work of Paul E. Barton (2009) is highly recommended for reading by any person interested in the history and the ups and downs of national education standards. Barton's publication is titled *National Education Standards: Getting Beneath the Surface*.

In the following section, the pros and cons of national education standards are addressed. Take a moment to think about your current position on the topic of national education standards for local schools. Might you be in favor of the concept, or are you non-supportive? Examine the following expressed pros and cons on the subject of national education standards and then think once again as to how you view the concept.

The Pros in Support of National Education Standards for Primary and Secondary Curricula

- National education standards may give us the ability to compare "apples to apples." As it is now, there are too many variations in the selection of standards among the states for any reasonable comparison.
- National standards offer continuity in education throughout the country and help students compete more effectively in a global society.
- National standards commonly are developed by professional personnel such as teachers, school administrators, and other experts in education and designed to prepare students for college and the workforce.
- National standards give parents, students, and teachers an accurate picture of what the student should be learning and provide an accurate picture of student progress throughout an academic career.
- Standards represent a first step of a building block with high-quality education outcomes.
- Present inconsistencies between the states do not provide an accurate picture of how schools are performing across the board.
- National standards are understandable and consistent in their statements.
- National standards serve additionally in their alignment with the common requirements for college entrance.
- National standards are valid and reliable since they are evidence based.
- National standards serve to build upon state standards that are already in place.

The Cons in Non-Support of National Education Standards for Primary and Secondary Curricula

- National standards represent more federal involvement in local school education and do not guarantee higher-quality education for students.
- Federal involvement in local school education will simply result in mudding the waters.
- Adding national education standards to local school programs will just result in too much bureaucracy in the education programs.
- National standards are really insufficient in giving an accurate picture of what students really learn.
- There has been no available assurance that national standards will serve to improve education for students.

- Some states already have better standards, and many others have similar standards already in practice.
- There is no agreement with the idea that holding schools accountable and providing benchmarks ensure that students get the education they need to be successful in life.
- Education improvement is expressed as a promise of standards but most likely will never be realized.
- Another weakness of national standards is that student academic achievement is based solely on external tests.
- National standards take away the autonomy of the classroom teacher, and motivation and creativity are endangered.
- The underlying flaw in national standards is the assumption that it is good for all!
- A false assumption concerning national standards is that it is assumed that high test scores are right because they get the student into good universities.
- The implementation of national standards for local school curriculum ignores the value of curriculum development at the local school level.
- Many teachers contend that implementing the national standards reduces the important factor of collaboration among the school faculty.

The matter of federal control of education certainly is not a new consideration.

We summarize our position on the topic at hand by indicating that national standards can have a positive impact on educational improvement in the nation's schools, but accompanying controls relative to what subjects are to be taught and how the subjects should be taught are out of order. America's local school programs have been influenced positively in the past by various commissions and groups. In 1918, the Commission on the Reorganization of Secondary Education set forth the influential Seven Cardinal Principles of Education. The recommendations of the Committee of Ten in (1892) reverberated throughout the halls of local schools, colleges, and universities nationally for many years, and its footprints on contemporary practices are in evidence today.

The early 1918 Seven Cardinal Principles of Education emphasized the needs for all youth: (1) health, (2) command of the fundamental processes, (3) worthy home membership, (4) vocational efficiency, (5) civic participation, (6) worthy use of leisure time, and (7) ethical character. Which need would you erase from the list today? What additional needs might be added? These general principles served to influence educational purposes for many years in textbooks used in local school classrooms of educational institutions. We contend that the major purposes of education programs belong in the hands of educators and other professionals and not within the channels of federal government.

RACIAL DISCRIMINATION AND THE FEDERAL GOVERNMENT

In discussing the educational controversies at the national level, it is necessary to examine the role of the federal government in education historically. It has been noted throughout this book that the U.S. Constitution does not mention education and has left this responsibility to individual states and people. Yet, it has been noted that today the federal government operates programs that touch every area and level of K–12 education.

The elementary and secondary departments within the federal Department of Education serve some 18,200 school districts and over 50 million students attending approximately 98,000 public schools and 32,000 private schools in the nation. Department programs also provide grants and other loan services and work-study assistance to more than 12 million postsecondary students (U.S. Department of Education, 2017). Does this service reveal deep federal involvement in education or something based on only a concern?

CONTROVERSIES RELATING TO RACIAL DISCRIMINATION IN EDUCATION

The topic of racial discrimination was discussed previously as it is debated at the local school and state levels. In those discussions, the inequities that exist in local schools for minority students were presented. Nevertheless, inequities in educational opportunities for many students within the various states have been a first-order concern at the national level.

Certainly, American morality and justice must favor the elimination of inequalities that exist in any education program. Yet, one has some difficulty in finding unbiased information; right-wing or left-wing sympathies commonly attend reports on the status of educational discrimination. Right-wing sources are generally associated with the Republican side of political matters, while the left-wing side is associated with the Democratic side. Media bias also comes into play. In any case, various reports do indicate that racism is still evident in American schools.

Earlier reports of the U.S. Department of Education during the presidency of Barack Obama stated that several discrepancies were evident in K–12 school practices. For example, according to the U.S. Education Department's findings, black students were being suspended or expelled from school at triple the rate of their white peers (Resmovits, 2014). In addition, this cited information stated that minority students were having less access to experienced teachers and also were attending schools where as many as 20 percent of the teachers were not sufficiently licensed and certificated.

Unbiased reports on the status of discrimination were not readily available to the public at the time of this writing in 2018. We make note of the fact that Joy Resmovits was formerly an educational writer for *HuffPost*. In any case, the basic question regarding educational discrimination remains relevant, "Do we need the federal government to control discrimination in public school education?" We submit that the federal government should fulfill its primary purpose: to support programs that promote effective student learning and preparing children and youth for their important participation in the nation's democratic society and giving assurance that each and every student has an equal chance to pursue the educational opportunities provided by the K–12 schools nationwide.

THE EDUCATIONAL CONTROVERSY OF SOCIAL PROGRAMS IN K–12 SCHOOLS

It is difficult to consider social programs as a pro or con topic. Unbiased research on the outcomes of social programs is virtually unavailable. The programs/social topics of Early Head Start, Head Start, abstinence education, free lunch program, Upward Bound, Job Corp, community learning centers, and others were pursued in relation to their educational outcomes. The con side of the federal involvements in education tends to reach the conclusion that none of the federal social programs have worked (Muhlhausen, 2014). In the case of Head Start and the academic preschool program, the most common comment of non-supporters is that these programs are too much too soon.

In all too many instances of publications on social services, the reporting group itself has come under serious criticism. This result appears to be the case of the Heritage Foundation that at one time in history was viewed as the "policy think tank" in its reports on important matters facing the nation. In fact, one report noted that former president Ronald Reagan passed out copies of the Foundation's work at his first cabinet meeting.

We do present one exception to the lack of research on social issues by describing the results of an early study by Anderson et al. (2003).

> Early childhood development programs are recommended on the basis of strong evidence of their effectiveness in preventing their delay of cognitive development and increasing readiness in retention in grade and placement in special education. Evidence was insufficient to determine the effects of these programs on social cognition and social risk behaviors. . . . Evidence was also insufficient to determine the effects of early childhood development programs on child health screening outcomes and family outcomes because too few comparative studies examined these outcomes. (40)

Once again, we allude to the lack of valid and reliable research on educational topics. The foregoing report by Anderson and others is an example of the kind of research needed in all cases of social programs and their education outcomes. The primary question here is, will education programs and their outcomes ever be assessed and evaluated by required, unbiased research professionals? Unless such valid and reliable research is done for each major social research program legislated at the national level, the time, effort, and high costs involved will continue to result in controversy and debate.

The "on and off" implementation and common dissolution of the many mandated social programs in K–12 school programs result in confusion and frustration on the part of school personnel and the general citizenry. In so many instances, the pluses, if any, of school social programs are identified and continued in place in the school's program. Other negative aspects of any program become chaff and fall through the cracks of ongoing change. Near the top of the list of controversies is the issue of social programs. Each entry to the program is based on the expressed purpose of helping children and youth to be better and do better. Their actual outcomes regarding the expressed purposes commonly remain unsettled.

THE FEDERAL EDUCATIONAL CONTROVERSY OF REDSHIRTING

Redshirting, is this a national education issue? The term *redshirting* is used in university sports programs whereby an athlete is held out of competition for a period of time, usually one year, to increase skills, extend eligibility, or wait for a year until a more experienced player leaves a position open. Such athletes usually continue to participate on the practice team but do not participate in the college or university regularly scheduled games. Redshirting has become a source of some of the most controversial debates surrounding education. As such redshirting is not only a local school concern.

Redshirting now is being practiced in education nationally most often at the kindergarten and first-grade levels. For example, kindergarten-aged children are withheld from entrance into school for the purpose of gaining time for additional growth. The extra time given before enrolling in school gives more time for mental, physical, and social development. That is, redshirting is meant to give the child more time to get ready for the "challenges" to be encountered in kindergarten and in the later grades. According to Katz (2000), redshirting occurs most often when the child's birthday is so close to the school entry cutoff dates that he or she would be among the youngest in their kindergarten class.

Educational Controversies at the Federal Level 107

In any case, redshirting has become an issue at the national level. The actual outcomes of redshirting remain controversial. Some research reports that redshirting does have certain advantages for what is referred to as the short term. On the other hand, there is some evidence that redshirting is not advantageous over the long term. The pros and cons regarding the practice of redshirting are set forth in the following section.

The Pros in Support of Redshirting in Education

- One study on life satisfaction showed that redshirting students had significantly higher levels of life satisfaction than those not redshirted.
- Redshirting locks children into patterns of achievement, while failure to do so results in discouragement and dissatisfaction.
- Redshirting places older members of the class in line for being chosen for the best learning opportunities.
- Redshirting is most prevalent among highly educated parents.
- Data show that kids with birthdays in the past three months of the year experience trouble with emotional strengths and maturity necessary for success at schools more than twice the rate of kids born in the first three months of the year.
- Redshirting has been found to have an impact on whether or not a student goes on to college.

The Cons against the Redshirting of Children in Education

- The research on the benefits of redshirts is "muddled."
- Overviews of redshirting show little to no academic advantages to the practice.
- The escalating demands for a more academic program in the early grades have given redshirting an unfortunate push in schools.
- It is commonly known that young children are disproportionately diagnosed with learning problems.
- In later life, it has been demonstrated that non-redshirted students earn more compensation than those who were redshirted.
- Redshirting has been found to have no impact on later life reception of advanced degrees.
- It has been found that redshirting shows little to no academic advantages.
- Redshirting, according to many teachers, makes it more difficult to meet the students' needs.
- Studies have been far less conclusive on long-term benefits of redshirting between those individuals who redshirt and those who do not. Data show that the gap vanishes by high school.

- There is evidence that the older kids get bored and fail to develop effective study skills.
- There are social consequences for holding kids back—friendships are broken when kids get into redshirting. There is more to a child's life than just academics; socializing with friends is lost when one moves from one grade to another.
- There is a flawed belief that the child who is older will win out. There is no evidence to support this belief.

We conclude the discussion on redshirting by referring to the comprehensive study published by *The New England Journal of Medicine* and reported by Christina Samuels. As reported by Samuels, "A newly released study published in the *New England Journal of Medicine* . . . found that kindergarten students who had turned 5 in the month before starting kindergarten were more likely to be diagnosed with attention deficit hyperactivity disorder than children who started kindergarten in the month that they turned 6" (Samuels, 2018). Deficit hyperactivity disorder is characterized by problems of paying attention, excessive activity, or difficulty controlling behavior, which is not appropriate for the person's age. Such research information is especially helpful to parents and others who are trying to make a decision on redshirting regarding their child.

Primary Chapter Ideas and Recommendations

- Many of the educational controversies at the federal level have long histories. The changes that take place in the political administration nationally over time have great influence on educational practices at the local level.
- The listing of educational controversies at the federal level is virtually unending. Most of federal educational debates find their way into educational controversies at the state and local levels.
- School choice and vouchers are high on the list of educational controversies at this time. Charter and private school programs are being supported by public funds to the detriment of the local public schools.
- The pros and con arguments related to the many education programs activities serve to clarify the various reasons that resolutions are difficult to achieve.
- Federal involvement in education tends to center on control. In order for the local school programs to receive federal support, it must comply with the federal requirements set forth.
- The common statement that education is a federal concern is an understatement. In most cases, federal concern is spelled "control."

- The lack of valid and reliable research is evident in virtually all controversial education matters. When scientific research is conducted, the results provide solution to the controversy in question.

Discussion Questions

1. Suppose you are in attendance at your local school's parent-teacher meeting. The question arises as to the matter of redshirting. Assume that you are the school's principal. Draft a statement that sets forth your position on the question.
2. This chapter, for the most part, presented a con position on the matter of federal involvement in K–12 education programs. What pro statements might you set forth that support federal involvement in education?
3. Education program activities such as vocational education, funding, curriculum, and others historically have been among the topics debated in the nation's schools. Even the local school curriculum has been debated in relation to the role of the federal government. Common Core is a prime example. The failure of the local schools scholastically is a topic of national concern. Give thought to how the federal government might be involved in resolving this controversy, if at all.
4. In a class or other group session, set up a debate on the topic of school choice. Use the primary debate procedures for debating the pro and con sides of the school choice controversy.
5. Resolved: The Need for National Standards for Local School Education Is Essential. Establish your personal list of pros or cons in relation to the support or non-support of the resolution set forth.

Case Study: Well, What Do We Do Now?

Dr. Ronn Black, superintendent of the Westbanks School District, was meeting with the school's site-based council at one of the local elementary schools. The topic of interest was the matter of pre-kindergarten education program activities. The site-based committee consisted of members of the school's parent-teacher association, school teachers, two business leaders, and two members of the school's administrative staff. Westbank School was one of ten elementary schools within the school district.

Two representatives of the parent-teacher association fully supported the need for initiating such a pre-kindergarten program. They cited several comments by the association's membership in favor of the program. Dylan Thomas, a business representative, stated that such programs had not shown positive empirical evidence of support. In fact, Thomas was of the opinion that such early education programs faded out in later years and actually made little or no difference educationally.

Tyler Scott, one of Westbank's sixth-grade teachers, commented that the costs of implementing such a program in all ten of the district's schools would be substantial. He wondered if the high cost would be wise in regard to what we know about such programs. In addition, pre-kindergarten teachers are hard to find, he noted.

Sara Morton, the sixth-grade student, said that his young sister had just turned to age four. He expressed a concern as to whether his sister would be able to sustain such a program outside the home. What would such a pre-kindergarten program teach? he asked.

Superintendent Black reiterated comments related to school district costs, but others insisted that costs were a secondary consideration. Education is what is of importance here, they responded.

Upon the adjournment of the meeting, Superintendent Black promised feedback on the matter in that he would take the matter into consideration. He was fully aware that the school district had to cut back on certain curriculum offerings due to the lack of financial support. In addition, Black had reservation on the preschool programs relative to research findings that program gains tended to fade out in the following years. Taking the matter to the school board would tend to open a controversial matter for the school district to contend. He wondered if he should take the matter to the school board for their deliberation or not.

Discussion Question

1. Assume the role of Superintendent Black and set forth your plan for following up on the preschool program matter. Is it best, for example, for you to turn over this program matter to the school board or perhaps ask supportive members of the parent-teacher association to take the lead on the matter? If, indeed, you have reservations and disfavor the addition of an early childhood program, would you respond directly to the Westbank School's Site-based Council?

REFERENCES

Anderson, L. M., et al. (2003). The effectiveness of early childhood development programs: A systematic Review. *American Journal of Preventive Medicine*, 24 (3S), 32–46.

Barton, P. E. (2009, June). *National education standards: Getting beneath the surface.* Policy Information Perspective, Educational Testing Service (ETS), Princeton, NJ.

Butler University (2017, September 17). *Banned books: Reasons for banning.* Libraries Center for Academic Technology. http://www,libguides.butler.edu/bannedbooks.

Cook, S. A., & Klay, W. E. (2014). Enlightenment ideas on educating future citizens and public servants. *Journal of Public Education Affairs*, 20(1), 45–55.

Dass, P. (2014). Deciphering Franklin D. Roosevelt's educational policies during the Great Depression (1933–1940). An unpublished doctoral dissertation. Scholarly Works@ Georgia State University. Deron Boyles, PhD, Doctoral committee chair.

Ho, S. (2018, June 10). Charter schools rebound after big California election loss. *U.S. News and World Report.* The Associated Press.

Katz, L. (2000). *Academic redshirting and young children.* ERIC Clearinghouse on Elementary and Early Childhood Education, University of Illinois at Champaign.

Leigh, J. (2014, September 18). *Ten reasons for banning books and 5 much better reasons not to.* www.punchnels.com/2014/09/18/10-reasons-for-banning-books-and-5-much-better-reasons-not-to/.

Muhlhausen, D. (2014, March 19). *Do federal social programs work?* The Heritage Foundation, Washington, D.C.

Norton, M. S. (2018). *The White House and education throughout the years: U.S. presidents' views and significant educational contributions.* Lanham, MD: Rowman & Littlefield.

Resmovits, J. (2014, March 21), *American schools are still racist government.* Minneapolis, MN: Walden University.

Samuels, C. (2018, November 29). Redshirting debate just got new fuel with ADHD study. *Education Week.* web blogs.edweek.org/edweek/speced/2018/ 11/redshirting_debate_and_ADHD_study.html.

U.S. Department of Education (2017, May 25). Federal student aid. ilibrary-Federal Work-Study (FWS) Program. https://ifap.ed.gov/ifap/by Topic.jsp?progam=78year=2017.

Wikipedia (2018, September 29). *Redshirting in education (academic).* https://en.Wickipedia.org/w/index/php?title=Redshirting_(academic)&oldid=8)734.

About the Author

Dr. M. Scott Norton has served as a secondary school teacher of mathematics; coordinator of curriculum for the Lincoln, Nebraska, School District; assistant superintendent for instruction; and superintendent of schools in Salina, Kansas, before joining the University of Nebraska as professor and vice-chair of the Department of Educational Administration and Supervision. He later served as professor and chair of the Department of Educational Administration and Policy Studies at Arizona State University, where he is currently professor emeritus.

His primary graduate research and instruction areas include curriculum and supervision, teaching methods, governance policy, instructional leadership, educational leadership, human resources administration, the assistant school principalship, research methods, organizational development, and competency-based administration.

He has published widely in national journals in such areas as teaching/instructional methods, curriculum development, organizational climate, instructional leadership, gifted student programs, and student retention.

Most recent textbooks authored by Dr. Norton include:

1. *Dealing with Change: The Effects of Organizational Development on Contemporary Practices* (2018).
2. *Guiding Curriculum Development: The Need to Return to the Local Level* (2016).
3. *Teachers with the Magic: Great Teachers Change Students' Lives* (2015).
4. *The Principal as a Learning Leader: Motivating Students by Emphasizing Achievement* (2013).

5. *The Principal as a Student Advocate: A Guide for Doing What's Best for All Students* (2012).
6. *A Guide for Educational Policy Development: Effective Leadership for Policy Development* (2017).
7. *Guiding the Human Resources Function: New Issues, New Needs* (2017).
8. *The Principal as Human Resources Leader: A Guide to Exemplary Practices for Personnel Administration* (2015).
9. *The Legal World of the School Principal: What Leaders Need to Know about School Law* (2016).
10. *The Changing Landscape of School Leadership: Recalibrating the School Principalship* (2015).
11. *The Whitehouse and Education through the Years: Presidents' Educational Views and Significant Educational Contribution* (2018).
12. *The Politics of Education* (2019).

Dr. Norton has received several state and national awards honoring his services and contributions to the field of educational administration from such organizations as the American Association of School Administrators, the University Council for Educational Administration, the Arizona Administrators Association, the Arizona Educational Research Association, Arizona State University College of Education Dean's Award for excellence in service to the field, President of the ASU College of Education Faculty Association, and the distinguished service award from the Arizona Information Service. He presently is serving as a member of the ASU Emeritus College Council.

Dr. Norton's state and national leadership positions have included service as executive director of the Nebraska Association of School Administrators, a member of the Board of Directors for the Nebraska Congress of Parents and Teachers, president of the Nebraska Council of Teachers of Mathematics, president of the Arizona School Administrators Higher Education Division, member of the Arizona School Administrators Board of Directors, staff associate of the University Council for Educational Administrators, treasurer of the University Council for School Administrators, Nebraska State Representative for the National Association of Secondary School Principals, member of the Board of Editors for the American Association of School Public Relations, and presently a governance council member for the Emeritus College of Arizona State University.

www.ingramcontent.com/pod-product-compliance
Lightning Source LLC
Chambersburg PA
CBHW030145240426
43672CB00005B/277